T0375566

HILDE LARSEN

From HELL to Inspired

A Journey from Severe Chronic Illness to Health and Vitality

FROM HELL TO INSPIRED

A Journey from Severe Chronic Illness to Health and Vitality

iUniverse books may be ordered through booksellers or by contacting:

iUniverse
1663 Liberty Drive
Bloomington, IN 47403
www.iuniverse.com
1-800-Authors (1-800-288-4677)

ISBN: 978-1-4917-9285-8 (sc)
ISBN: 978-1-4917-9290-2 (hc)
ISBN: 978-1-4917-9284-1 (e)

Library of Congress Control Number: 2016905979

Print information available on the last page.

iUniverse rev. date: 4/21/2016

CONTENTS

PART 4   THE POWER WITHIN

PREFACE.

Writing this book has been a deep healing experience for me. I have known for many years that I wanted to write this journey down on paper. People have been asking me about my personal self-lived experiences, so I knew this day was coming. For a very long time I have been holding back, waiting for the perfect time, not even knowing what that would look like. I can clearly see that there was simply more information that I needed to gather, for it to be a part of this book.

From constantly loading up on information, experimenting and finding more and more truth, I was shown that this was the time. This was the time to focus on my writing, and to let my story be told. It is with a combination of enthusiasm and feeling naked, that I share something this personal with all whom will find interest in my passion for true healing. My eagerness to Inspire through sharing cannot be held back. Once I started to write, there was no stopping the process. It was like opening a floodgate. I sat down, opened my Mac, and it all came flowing. The time was right.

As I kept writing, I realized that I was writing two books. There was too much information to fit into one single book. It would be too much to take in at one time, and it would simply be too compact, or an information overload. I was led to separate *my story* from a *step by step practical knowledge book*. This way, after reading *"from HELL to Inspired"*, you will be able to move on to a separate one, which will hold all the recipes, the tricks and the special personal tips for your own journey. *"Know the Truth and get Healthy"* is all about YOUR path, how YOU will get to where you want to be. Although a lot of what I have done to be living my dreams is between this books covers, the book *"Know the Truth and get Healthy"*, has the complete step by step plan all laid out for you.

The process of writing everything under such an intense flow and passion, has been such a great learning process. It could not be stopped, and thanks to some amazing helpers, it all came together beautifully.

Thank you Helge, my trusted honest and first line proof reader. Always eager to dive in to the new material.

Thank you Elena for showing up at the perfect time, and for your compassionate work with my text. You have been such a blessing.

This book will also be published in Norwegian, my native language. It might seem strange why I chose to write my first book in English, but I really felt it was important for my story to reach as many as possible. My passion has always been to Inspire, and now is no different. If this book will inspire you to go after your own healing and health, I feel blessed and humbled.

THANK YOU.

The gratitude that fills me is beyond words. It reaches out to all of you who are reading this book; my tribe, my family, my friends and my spirit guides.

During my darkest times, when living in this body seemed absolutely not doable, I still had the hope and the vision that this day would come. The day where I would be able to share my story, to serve, help and to guide others towards a healthy and amazing life.

I want to thank my children Therese and Thomas, who never lost faith in me, and who always cheered me on. They truly lost their old mum, and gained a brand new one. The love I have for them, and the honor it is for me to be their mother, most likely saved me more than once.

Thank you Helge, my dear husband, for walking beside me, for being my biggest fan, and my partner in crime. Thank you for growing with me. Thank you for challenging me, and for loving me. I love you forever.

The birth of my soul mate, muse, and my love, Mia, my granddaughter, has shown me the responsibility we all hold. We are called to step forth, to protect and to take responsibility. We have been called to let the little ones feel safe and loved. She was born while I was very sick and tired, and came into my life like a bright shining star. Mia, you are the light and the one who leads the way, and I will always continue to learn from you. Your spirit has shown me how connected we all are, and how much love is present. I love you and your little brother Emil beyond words, and I thank you for coming into my life. Thank you for giving me even more purpose.

My best friend May, who kept knocking on my door until it opened, never giving up on reaching out to me. You made me stronger, more determined and focused. Your amazing kindness and empathic nature kept me sane.

I want to thank every person that I never met, who was giving me support on the internet when my social network and world fell apart. YOU were my lifeline, my hope and my inspiration. This was before Facebook, and the forums were all we had. Thank you Dr. Kenneth Sutter, for spending all that time on online forums helping people like me. You saved my life.

There are too many people whose wisdom I have tapped into to mention them all. Dr. Wayne Dyer, Eckhart Tolle, Louise Hay, Bruce Lipton, Arnold Ehret, Gregg Braden, Deepak Chopra, Doreen Virtue are just some of those who have contributed to my growth and personal evolvement. One person stands out, and has a very special place in my heart; Dr. Robert Morse, my dear friend, you still keep empowering me with your wisdom. Your knowledge and eagerness to share and help, is changing this world. I feel blessed to know you, dear soul.

I am humble to be able to share this story, and my intention is to let you all know that you can change your health and your life. Health is natural, and no matter how sick you are, how lost you feel, and how tired you feel, KNOW that there is hope.

My life has been filled with a whole new perspective, an inner peace, and a feeling of true freedom. For that, I thank God and the infinite guidance. I have been guided and supported from a high power of wisdom and truth, and will be grateful for that, until the day I am no longer here, in this body.

Writing this book has brought back memories that I had been putting aside. Painful stories, fear, hopelessness and despair. Revisiting this journey, this walk of life, has brought me even more healing, and for that I thank you God.

Thank you,

Thank you,

Thank you.

INTRODUCTION.

About 8 years ago, I decided I was done. I was done being sick, and I was done struggling. I was so filled up on medications, hospital visits, anxiety and pain, that I decided to just stop. I had been diagnosed with severe rheumatoid arthritis several years before, and was heavily medicated - I was told that I was a "severe" case. The diagnosis of Lyme disease, ulcers, anxiety and more, was not helping my suffering soul and spirit.

The medical society tells you, you will be sick for the rest of your life, and that medications will be your only hope to live as "normal" as possible. What they do not tell you, is a very different story, and what they do not know - might kill you.

Well, this one day about 8 years ago, I had had enough. I remember thinking, "I will stop all medications and just lie here until I get well, or I die." I really did not care which, as long as what I was experiencing stopped.

From being a mother, a sister, a wife, a business owner, an athlete, and a friend, I just became sick. My world changed overnight. I was alone, and I did not know what to do to save myself. As soon as I stopped the medications that made me very ill, I got more ill. Now, my body was showing me just how sick I really was.

A long journey started, a lonely one, filled with pain, fear, and hopelessness. Every day was a battle for survival. My heart did not beat regularly for years. I was bedridden, and could not even go to the bathroom by myself, not for several years. I could not open my mouth or chew foods, as my jaw was too inflamed. I often prayed that I would not wake up in the morning. Watching your body deteriorate, and your joints slowly cripple, is a challenge for the mind, the emotions and the soul.

Something inside me told me that health was there, if I would just let it come forth. I studied all day, every day. I spent all my time searching the internet, reading books and watching videos. Slowly my way of thinking changed, my diet changed, and my connection to my spirit opened up.

Friends left, and new amazing souls came into my life. It is hard for family members and friends to understand, and to know how to help when someone gets very sick. Change is often felt as a scary thing, so never blame them for not being there. They do not know any better.

Along this journey I have seen stones turn into diamonds, I have seen life become magical, and I have seen my body transforming before my very eyes. How amazing is that? As I look back, I can see the true gift in my ongoing journey from HELL to Inspired. I made a choice, and I followed my inner guidance. The gift was hidden to me, but is no more. It is now shining as my true purpose.

I am still evolving, getting better, learning, and experiencing the amazing connection with nature and God's force. Yet, the biggest gift of all, is to see how my knowledge and experience is helping others find their true health, and their inner power!

Now, all these years later, my heart is beating perfectly, and the anxiety is gone. My digestion is back to normal after 20 years of ulcers, and my skin looks better than it has in years.

I am not stopping until my body is 100% healthy - and beyond! And they said it could not be done! NEVER let anybody tell you that. Not your family, friends, NOBODY! This has been my biggest gift, and I would not be without this journey.

I have awakened, and found my inner balance.
I have found joy and appreciation, for all of creation.
I have learned to love myself.
I am letting go of everything that does not serve me.
I am no longer part of the illusion of drama or pain.

The *now* moment is where the magic is, and for those of you that struggle with health issues, KNOW that it is in your hands to change. Your body is made to be healthy, it's what it is designed to be. It is all vibration, and it's all connected. Stop poisoning it, and start nurturing it. Change your thoughts, and your emotions will follow. Clear out the toxins from your body, and the mind will clear. Your vibration and your consciousness will rise.

Align your focus with the solution, not with the problem!

Speak what you want, and expect it to happen. *Be* the change you want to see, and love yourself the whole way there. Nobody is perfect, in fact perfection is an illusion, it does not exist. YOU are the perfect YOU!

So, my dear reader, you who have found this book, stand up for what you believe in! Find support and stay focused. Health and happiness really is a choice. Spend time in nature, connect with your inner-self, and trust the process.

I will take you through my journey back to life, to joy and true inspiration. I am using my own words, and my heart felt intention is to reach your heart and promote faith and inner connection. Your health is *your* choice, and I hope that by reading about my journey, you will get inspired to take back your power! We all create our own reality, and *you* are God also.

If I can do this, *you* can do this. I hope that you, by reading through this walk of mine, will be inspired to live your life to the fullest, and to never, ever give up. Not on anything. These are my own experiences, and the story is meant to lift and empower you. This is your time, and this is your moment.

My greatest wish is that this book will reach out to someone who needs the support and the encouragement that I hope it to be.

This is my story and my blessing, and to make your journey as easy as possible, my next book *Know the Truth and get Healthy* is there for you when you are ready.

Be blessed in the flow of joy and bliss, always!

Power up on LIFE!

MEDICAL ADVICE/DISCLAIMER:

This book, with its opinions, suggestions and references, are based on the author's personal experience and is for personal study and research purposes only. This book is about health and vitality, not disease. The author makes no medical claims. Information in this book is not meant to treat or diagnose any disease. This is not medical advice, but a sharing of personal experiences.

The information, ideas, and suggestions in this book are not intended as a substitute for professional medical advice. Before following any suggestions contained in this book, consult your physician. Neither the author nor the publisher shall be liable or responsible for any loss or damage allegedly arising as a consequence of your use or application of any information or suggestions in this book.

Taking responsibility for oneself is a great message to take from reading this book. This is for educational and inspirational use only. Self-empowering is a great asset to any health regime, and it is of great value for every aspect of life. Seek freedom from disease, seek healing.

PART ONE
LIFE UNPOLISHED

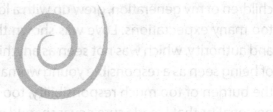

Chapter 1

Life is always
speaking to you.

Before I get to the topic of this book, I want to share with you a short revisit of my background. I will not bore you with a long childhood story, nor do I believe in dwelling on the past. No matter how our childhood has influenced us, it is never too late to have a happy one. We are all affected by our past. Everything we hear, process, and emotionally react to, is affecting our belief system, our behavior and our cells. The cells have memory, and will store every incident, happy or otherwise. Still, two different people will never react in the same way to the same situation. Our whole blueprint, our genetic composition and our past-life experiences, are believed to influence how we react to and respond to outer stimuli.

Growing up in Norway in the '60-s and '70-s, was safe and fairly harmonious for me. I am the oldest of three sisters, and went through what most first-borns did at that time. I believe that most first-born children of my generation, grew up with a lot of responsibilities and too many expectations. Love was shown through discipline, rules and authority, which was not seen as anything but healthy. The fun of being seen as a responsible young woman felt like it outweighed the burden of too much responsibility, too soon. What shaped my personality, that I made sure never shaped my own children`s, is the lack of being told *I love you*. The lack of feeling loved is a deep and often many life-times old rooted issue. I was by no means alone being brought up this way. I believe that most of my generation lacks the general feeling of being loved.

I never missed anything besides this, growing up. Both my parents worked for most of my childhood. We lived in a great house in a friendly and safe neighborhood. It was truly a happy place to grow up, and our house had all the space that we needed

I had to grow up too soon though, and became the independent *good girl* that one could always rely on. That girl that people expected the most from. The one most likely to be held accountable. I never got into trouble, and my grades in school were always good. I had a lot of friends, and I have so many fond memories from my youngest days. My parents did the best they knew how, and raised three women to be proud of. Looking back at my upbringing, I can see that the things that programmed me for stress and ill health, also prepared me for my journey of awakening. By this I mean that my independence, my ability to endure and be strong, would be what I needed to get through what was coming much later down the road.

As a child, I would say my health was within the *normal* range. Minor things like rashes and insensitivities occurred, but never resulted in hospitalization or illness. I was an active gymnast, and very energetic. I played the piano, and was great at artistic drawings. All of my friends were healthy growing up. We spent a lot of time outdoors, and were constantly physically active. This was before cell phones and computers (I know, hard to even imagine) so when we needed to speak, we walked over to each other's houses. When we were together, we talked, played, and were truly there in the present moment. I often think about how our parents had to really trust that we were ok, with no means of connecting with us when we were out of the house for whole days at a time. In the light of this, the general stress level back then was much lower than it is today. TV was something that we watched for an hour a day at the most, and soda and potato chips were a treat we enjoyed on Saturdays only.

From when I was about ten years old, we spent our summers at our amazing summer place. There was no running water in the cabin, so we used well-water. This was still-water, and one summer I was overwhelmed with a terrible body rash. My parents ended up having the water analyzed by the city authorities, and the result was alarming. The bacteria load was off the charts, so high, they were wondering if those who had been drinking this water were even still alive. I was the only one in my family with this reaction, showing how even back then, my body was not handling toxins very well. I was already overloaded.

Our early habits, our experiences and our genetic composition, are what we bring with us into adulthood, and for me it was no different. The weakness caused by consuming dairy products, meat and gluten, was showing itself through my health before the decade had passed. The symptoms would slowly sneak up on me.

Processed foods were filling up our plates at a high speed. I remember when pizza came, and instantly became the Saturday treat at our house. It was part of a fast growing food industry, mowing down health. We were highly and indiscriminately vaccinated from head to toe. There were no questions asked. Any authority was highly respected, and no one ever questioned the opinion of a doctor, not a *real* doctor anyway.

My teens got highly disrupted by my family moving. I had been in the same environment my whole life, and I was very grounded where I was. Having to leave all my friends was very traumatic, to say the least. Starting a new school at the age of fifteen, knowing no one, was almost too much to handle. I still do not remember the actual move. Sometimes our body locks away the memories that are too painful to keep. I was grieving, and I felt lost. I think this is when my lonely, inner-strength first revealed itself. A survival mode kicked in, and some of my childish spirit got lost in the process. It was like I moved from childhood to adulthood overnight. I lived, and found new friends. I kept in contact with some of the old ones, and my social life picked up fairly quickly.

I developed a need to do good. It is a very common need. *We expect more from you*, is what I remember my mother telling me. I started to expect only the best from myself also, thinking if I did not do good, I was not good enough. The cells in our body listen to everything we think, say and feel, so this became my truth. I expected more from *me*.

Leading up to what seems to have been the final breakdown of my body, looking back, was me not listening. My body was trying so hard to let me know what was going on, but I was too busy, too ignorant and completely out of touch with it. I was on my way to disaster, full speed, and totally unaware that I was.

Having been groomed to be a nice girl, with the highest expectations of myself, I was ready for a do-it-all adulthood. I was sure that managing everything by myself was a good thing. Working hard no matter what, and always being the center of attention, was who I was. Or so I thought. I was so deeply invested in the *doing and performing* mode, as most people are today, that the contact with my inner voice was disconnected. I was so unavailable, that no sign from my body could get through to me.

I left for Florida at the age of eighteen, to study and to work. I was ready to stand on my own, and to explore the world. Florida was a long way from home, and my education was in a foreign language. Even though there were some amazing people around me that I could call family, and I was never alone - I was the accountable adult in my life. I carried with me the programming of having to be at the top of my class (of course), and it worked out very well. I was an A+ student, and I simply loved it! Don't get me wrong - there is nothing wrong with being best that you can be. Being good is a great thing. Being able to use your talents is a true blessing, but for me and many like me, we do not see the underlying force that drives us. I was absolutely a person that wanted to please others. From always having had the high childhood expectations, I carried with me the need to perform and to please someone besides myself. We are often carrying the programming of thinking that being good at something defines who we are. All humans have the same basic needs, to be loved, to feel included in a community, and to be recognized. Children will do anything to feel loved and to get recognized. If we carry with us that uncertainty, that we are not loved unless we perform, we will try to compensate for it in our adulthood. We will try to achieve, to be seen and to be recognized. I was now doing just that. Like so many others, I was burning my fuel trying to over-achieve at any task, and to keep a facade that was as close to perfect as possible. Perfect is important, right?

My strengths became my own worst enemies. Endurance, high achievement ability, a strong constitution, will and determination. Those are the very same abilities that would save my life many years later. Now, they kept me going, long past any sign of pain and uneasiness. My strengths kept me going full speed, even though my inner voice was getting anxious. My body was trying to reach me by sending out smaller signs of dis-ease along the way. Small subtle signs of stress.

I left Florida, and went through a traumatic period of separation and confusion. A long love-relationship ended, and a new one began. My life was turned upside down, but I was steaming ahead. Before long, I was in a new house, married, and pregnant with my daughter. My stomach had started to give me some troubles. Constipation and ulcers. Still, I was living my life like everybody else. I gave birth to two beautiful children, had a wonderful loving husband, a house, cars, a boat, and I was starting my own business.

The picture of a great life, and one that I kept living for many years. We became the regular family that did it all; vacations, parties, after school activities, working and exercising. The typical stress-inducing, achieving, and disconnecting lifestyle that most of us know so well. The type of life where you are trying to fit into an invisible box by constantly doing and striving to achieve.

My adult life seemed great for a very long time. My education as an interior architect, which I absolutely loved, my marriage and my wonderful children kept me going. I opened my own business, and was able to keep up the pace. That is the way we do life, right? We go after that *perfect* image of what life should look like. Feelings of stress might arise, and the body might be showing symptoms of disease, but that is only a part of living. The body is not what most people regard as the guiding force, the mind is. Our thoughts and analytical abilities can easily be our biggest enemy. The mind is a great tool, don't get me wrong, but it can also turn on us. Every single time the mind tries to go against the soul`s manifestation throughout the body - the body will let us know. If we do not listen, it will keep screaming louder. It will try to get us to listen in any way that it can. I know all about this, and I do not recommend turning the deaf ear. My experience has been painful and long standing, and I wish that your path will benefit from mine.

Apart from having my tonsils out at three (which was very common), and some allergic reactions and rashes, like the one from the well water, I was functioning as well as the next girl growing up, really. There was no indication that I was going to be experiencing a total loss of health and vitality. I was living my life like most people as far as diet and environment goes. My diet was typically Norwegian; based on milk, bread, potatoes and animal flesh. Very close to most Western diets. Although there wasn't much junk-food on our plates growing up, we grew accustomed to the processed dairy and sugar-based foods that invaded every supermarket. This diet slowly contributed to my health going downhill. We drank milk straight from the bottle, and were strong believers that milk was good for us. These beliefs, together with my lack of nutritional understanding, made me a ticking bomb just waiting to go off. I was going to keep ticking for years - in fact, for so many that I eventually got used to the ticking sound.

Chapter two:

The downhill spiral.

remember very well when the obvious journey towards Hell started. It was my first experience with an ulcer. I was about twenty-two years old, and I had just eaten raw lamb. Yes, raw lamb! This is a typical holiday treat in Norway, a leg of lamb that has been salted and then hung to dry. The pain was unbearable, and I had to be taken to the ER. At the hospital there was nothing special about the findings; No one questioned a young, and apparently healthy woman having an acid burn in her stomach. I was sent home with a prescription in my hand, and that was that. I had no idea at the time, that this was the first incident in what would later become years and years of a physical body desperately trying to show me that something was very wrong. That I was on my way to what I call Hell. It was the start of fifteen years of recurrent ulcers, constipation and stomach pains.

A year after the raw-lamb-incident, I had just gotten pregnant with my first child, Therese. Life until then had been busy, fun, eventful and stressful. It was the life I had grown accustomed too. I was the trustworthy, kind, do it all, know it all girl. I was always on call, trying to be perfect. I was trying to make everyone proud, except myself.

I am now told that I have a full blown ulcer, and that I need to be medicated. From that point on, my doctor became my best friend. He was the go-to person for relief and support, and he gave me any drug that I asked for, mostly. He put me on Nexium, an antacid drug, and I was constantly carrying Titralac with me. Anyone who has had gastrointestinal troubles during the eighties or nineties, knows what I am talking about; It is an acid reduction liquid medicine, over the counter and very popular. I would try anything to ease the symptoms.

I could hardly eat anything without feeling pain, not even drink a glass of water. Looking back, it's amazing to see that nothing at all was known or shared about diet. No one asked me what I was consuming. No one questioned that I was drinking diet coke as my main liquid-source, topped off with coffee, and beer during the weekends. No one wanted to know what I was eating, to find that Cheese Doodles were my favorite snack. The doctors were purely medicine-focused, and sadly most of them still are. That is what they are trained to do, I just wish I knew - and had been shown, that there are alternatives out there. Back then there was no Internet, and searching for alternative solutions on my own was not an easy option. Thankfully, I do see some brave and amazing doctors today, awakening to healing and regeneration, and I bow to them for doing so.

I started seeing an amazing reflexologist not long after my stomach symptoms, and that probably opened the door for my future interest in natural healing modalities. My unstable ulcerous stomach followed me through my pregnancies and beyond. Always lingering behind the scene. My journey was mapped, and I had no idea what turn, or route, it was going to take. Every choice that we make is writing our story, and every thought, emotion and action, has a reaction. Cause and effect.

My health issues never set me back as far as my performance in life, or so I believed. It never slowed me down as far as creating more things and stressful situations. It slowly weakened my inner spirit, but it never slowed me down. A curse and a blessing at the same time. I was able to be a mother, a wife, a sister, a daughter, a friend, a worker and a team-leader. I was able to keep up my appearance and my tasks. But I also remember lying on the bathroom floor after taking an enema, in so much pain that I blacked out. Constipation meant enema. Going 3-4 days with no bowel movement was normal for me. I had no idea that the bowel should move every single day, and even 2-3 times a day when healthy. So, enemas became my friends, even though I hated them. Painful and stressing is what they were to me. The enema bags that you can get online, and fill with water, are not the kind that I had my hands on back then. These were small plastic bottles with a saline solution that they sold at the pharmacy. You had to lie down on your side, on the bed, and try to maneuver this thing up your rectum. It was messy and frustrating. I was trying to mask a symptom, while the constipation continued. I was trying to take care of the result, not the cause.

Back to me being young and pregnant, newly married and very happy. The baby wanted to come out after about twenty weeks, so I was put on medications to keep me from giving birth too early. I was so sick, and I remember feeling like something was very wrong with me. Our daughter Therese was born a month early, so tiny and beautiful. A perfect little girl. She was such a blessing, and life found balance in an unbalanced situation.

I also had severe sciatica when Therese was little, and I was lying on the floor for weeks at a time. The terrible back pain and immobility would follow me for years, and I became a trusted client at my chiropractor's office. I remember well one time while I was running an aerobics studio with a former friend, and had to drive myself to work almost flat on my back. I was not able to walk, or to sit. More medications were added to my medicine cabinet. Somadril, a muscle relaxant no longer on the market, was mixed with painkillers for optimal effect. Don't get me wrong, I was not running after pills or getting addicted, but the truth is - I was not afraid to pop a pill. I had no reluctance to eating any drug given to me. Somadril took the edge off everything, and kept me going against the current.

We were blessed with a son, Thomas, less than three years after Therese was born. I had a miscarriage just months before conceiving him, so needless to say, the pregnancy was much celebrated. The celebration was short-lived, as yet again my body tried to reject the fetus. This time it was worse; my body was not ready for another large task like child birth.

One night, terrible pain was building up on the right side of my body. It was getting unbearable, and we called the hospital. I was told to take some pain killers and try to get some sleep. They were telling me how many pills I could take, being pregnant. There was no way I could rest or sleep, and the pain got so bad, I was picked up by an ambulance in the middle of the night. My husband could not leave our sleeping daughter, so I had to go by myself. I felt lost and afraid. They kept talking about the baby, and I kept telling them the pain had nothing to do with the pregnancy. I felt the pain was coming from my right kidney. Still, I was put in the gynecology ward. After two days, they listened to me and did an ultrasound of my kidneys. A kidney stone had passed, some little ones were still present, and I got an answer to my terrible pain. The story of how important healthy kidneys are, is also about to be told. This was what was showing itself without me knowing. The kidneys had tried to speak to me for a while, and would keep on trying for years to come. No one would listen. They were desperate, and no one would pick up the signs or signals. No one, least of all me, would even think to listen to the body's attempts to tell us all that it was heading for a major crash.

I was confined to bed for the last four months of this pregnancy. Medicated yet again, and bedridden. It was a stressful time for our little family. My husband was working to put food on the table, and our little girl had to be put in daycare. I spent my days reading in bed, putting on an enormous amount of weight, and holding on to a massive amount of water-weight. I remember them giving me diuretics after giving birth, even though they were very hesitant of doing that. My body was holding on to about twenty-two pounds (ten kilos) of water, and it was not leaving on its own. My kidneys were about to shut down, but no one reacted to that fact. Nothing was done, except to give me more drugs. I took them, the water left, and I could go on with my not very healthy life. Thomas was born feet first, and I broke my tailbone during delivery. It set me back for a while, but I was soon back on my feet, being an aerobics instructor, slim and ready. I took both children with me to my aerobics classes from the time Thomas was about 4 months old. I was constantly on the move. I am amazed at how much a body can endure, and still function at a level we see as *normal*. I was considering myself normal this whole time. Everyone had some sort of ailment, some sort of pain or discomfort. I could see that I had more than most, but I was strong, I could handle it. I was brought up not to complain, and to not seek comfort or compassion. I could do this, I could override my symptoms, and I did, for a long time.

My body was not on my team, so to speak. It was weaker than me. I saw my body as being off, *and I was doing my best not to listen to it. It was slowing me down now, and I would not have it. This is definitely why I had to experience my body going from whispering, to talking, to yelling, to slamming me over the head before I would listen.*

Then came a time of much stress on many different levels. We were building a new house, I was starting my own business, and

I was instructing aerobics and spinning classes in the evenings. Something had to give. I was getting severe hives, and experienced a serious anaphylactic shock. The Emergency Medical team had to come to my house in the middle of the night, to give me a shot of Prednisone. A shock like that can be life threatening. My lips and throat had started to swell, so the red lights were on. After the incident, I was told to always carry steroids in my purse, should it happen again. I did, and my travel bag had yet another drug to bring on our vacations. (There were already the stomach pain medications, the pain killers and the muscle relaxers.)

I can clearly see a turning point, a point when things started to go down-hill faster. It was after I was bitten by a tick in the summer of 1994. My body was not up for anything that needed even a little bit of strength. My inner terrain was an inviting environment for any little critter that needed a place to grow and have fun. I was bitten on my left instep, on top of my foot. I did not even notice until a few days later, as the bite was underneath the top strap of my sandals. We had been celebrating summer solstice with my husband`s family. I never gave a thought to being bitten by a tick. I had read about it, but I had been running barefoot, outdoors, all my life. I am still not sure one should be too concerned by those little critters, but this little tick-bite changed a lot for me. I was heading for the wall, bite or no bite, but it pushed me into another level of suffering. I got a large rash and a typical bulls-eye at the place of the bite. I knew I had to see a doctor. I was prescribed antibiotics, which is the typical medical protocol. I did a course of 2 weeks, and did not think more of it, not for many, many years.

The digestive troubles were now in company of several other symptoms. My eyes got acutely inflamed, and I was prescribed some cortisol eye-drops. They took the edge off, for a while. I used the drops for years, as my eyes kept flaring with an intense redness, soreness and burning. They were inflamed and irritated. I was burning up from head to toe. My doctor was starting to get frustrated by all my symptoms, as he had no real answer to offer me. What could I do, besides take my prescribed medicine and live my life the best I could?

I was experiencing everything from urinary tract infections to pneumonias. I remember one time, the children were around 7 and 10 years of age, and we had been on a weekend trip to Copenhagen with my in-laws. When we got to the airport going back home, I was getting severe bladder pain. I felt I had to pee non-stop. I was taken to an airport medical doctor, and he gave me a round of antibiotics on the spot. I thought nothing of it. All I wanted was to get out of pain, so that I could carry on with my life. I was suppressing the symptoms and hurting my kidneys even more. Antibiotics are like poison to any kidneys, and mine were already weak. How could I know? I couldn`t. I have no idea how I managed to run a business during these years. I just don't know, but the strength of a person is amazing. In my case, the determination I obviously had to not listen to my body, is the same determination that would later save my life.

I was struggling on, not getting much support for the need to slow down. I did not have a support system at that time. I did not have anyone in my circle that would tell me to take better care of myself. Most of us sadly don't. Dear reader, if you are considering a change, that is where I would start. If I had the chance to change anything along the way, I would be more open and authentic with a circle of close friends. Besides me not being so stubborn and absorbed with my appearance and image, I would make sure I had that close circle of good friends that had my back. Someone that would tell me it was ok to slow down, and that what I was experiencing was real. When you are brought up not being taught that it is ok to take care of *you*, and that complaining about pain and health is of no interest, you carry with you a pattern. You carry with you a program that tells you to keep on going no matter what. This is also why no man is an island. We need to lean on each other. I am in great appreciation of this lesson, and the fact that I have had the opportunity to grow and learn. This lesson alone is of greater value than what is perceivable. It is the lesson of togetherness, yet still being responsible for ourselves, 100%.

This reminds me of when I was working one of my first jobs as an interior architect. I got pregnant with Therese while working there, and I was called to my boss' office shortly after. He was yelling at me, telling me that he had hired me because he thought I was a hard worker, not someone who got pregnant and sick. I was devastated. It gave me more of what I already believed; I knew this, I should please others, step up in every situation, and not listen to myself. *I* was always the least prioritized by my own concern. The trick is though, that I was never perceived as such, because of my strength. Also - keep in mind that this is a pattern of the subconscious, and not something that I was living consciously. I was not seeing myself as anything but totally in charge and on top of things. That is a big part of the whole, that most often we cannot see our own patterns. I most certainly couldn't see mine. I was experiencing getting yelled at for being pregnant, and that this was perceived as not being optimal for a hard worker. I was still being conditioned to appear as a *top of the class performer*, no matter what. I was still being told what was expected of me. This episode stayed with me though it left a sadness within me. I somehow *knew* that it was ok to be vulnerable, pregnant and happy, I *knew* being pregnant was not the same as being weak.

A person that believes that he needs to keep up appearances no matter what, has a way of hiding anything that can be related to as a weakness.

To me, being sick was programmed as the equivalent of being weak and *less than*. My whole life was showing me this very *truth*. Being sick meant not being able to perform, and being seen as weakened and broken. At all costs, I would not let anyone see how sick I was, or how much pain I was in. I was strong, that was who I was, and I held on to that with all that I had.

The ulcers hit a high around my 35th time around the sun. As you know, I had had them on and off for years, but now it hit the fan. I could no longer live with the constant pain that came with it. I had been scheduled to do a colonoscopy and a gastroscopy both. My doctor was frustrated, and out of ideas, so why not do some tests again. This was not my first time doing either of them, but I had found a private specialist to do the testing this time around. I was getting worn out by living in pain, and I was grasping at straws. My body had started to show me other signs of not being in optimal health also, like the reoccurring urinary tract infections. On top of this the inflamed eyes continued, my back was hurting me, and I was constantly constipated. I never felt well.

This time, the gastroscopy test was conclusive. They found the *Helicobacter Pylori* bacteria, and believe it or not, I was happy. *H. pylori* are spiral-shaped bacteria that grow in the digestive tract and have a tendency to attack the stomach lining. After being present for many years, the bacteria can cause sores, called ulcers, in the lining of the stomach or the upper part of your small intestine. I am suspecting that our well-water from way back then, is where I invited these germs inside. They can live within our system for a very long time before any symptoms are manifested.

Now they would finally know how to fix me once and for all. This was great news at the time. Remember, I had been struggling with the pain and the ulcers for all of my adult life, and now they were telling me they knew how to fix it! They finally found what was wrong with my stomach, and they would fix it! I celebrated!

I had no reason to doubt the specialist, and I was very happy when he prescribed a course of nothing less than 3 different antibiotics. Cipro being one of them. Cipro is a drug known to have many serious side effects, a very nasty and strong antibiotic. Today I know how devastating this was to my health. The round of antibiotics did not take away my pain, even though the bacteria was supposedly gone. My doctor gave me another round, and to make sure - I took it! Now, after this, I was again able to carry on down the heavily trafficked road that was my life. Me and my work, my training and my high performing social life, would all be able to carry on while I was in great pain and despair.

I had so many things to be grateful for though, and now I was going to get well. The doctor told me this round of medicine would fix all of my stomach pains and symptoms. I truly believe that this doctor did what he thought was the best thing to do at the time, I am sure of it. *But* – those heavy rounds of antibiotics were no monkey business for this body, and left me exhausted and fatigued. I had been killing off most off the bacteria in my body, both the good ones *and* the not so good ones. I was suppressing the symptoms even more, and hurting my adrenal and kidney functions. All without me or anyone else knowing. I would know this much later, and can only be sorry that the knowledge of the adrenal and kidney connection to health was not out there.

After this, my energy levels were going down. It was getting harder to keep all of my appointments. It was getting harder to find peace and relaxation. It was like I was in a constant stress-mode, like my body got stuck in *busy-gear*. I was looking for an escape, and I found it in travelling, parties and anything that would distract me from myself. It was not comfortable being in my body, and I needed to forget and numb the symptoms. My soul and spirit were speaking loudly, but I wasn't listening. I did not know what listening to myself was. No one ever taught me how.

I was now secreting liquids from one of my breasts. Can you imagine? My breast was overflowing with internal acids, and nobody knew this fact. Nobody could tell me what was coming out of me, or why. There was no explanation. I remember I was freaking out. I was sent to another specialist, and he had me scheduled for a mammography to look for tumors. After that I was scheduled for an ultrasound as a follow up. Nothing could be found at that time. There was no answer to why my breast was leaking grey fluid, and I was starting to feel like I was going crazy. I was spending my time going from doctor's office to doctor's office, while working all day. To keep everything at full speed ahead, I was working in the evenings as well. I was taking care of my home, my children, my husband and wearing my high heels while doing it.

I got used to running to and from doctor's appointments during lunchtime, while I was running my business the best I could. I think my friends and family got used to me constantly not feeling good. It became a kind of normal. At least that is what I believe; Sometimes we get so used to how things are, we do not see that something is very off.

I was so focused on my everyday tasks and commitments, and to show just how lost I was in the race of life, I even had breast implants put in. Oh yes, that was me. My health was going downhill, and I spent my energy changing my appearance. I was following the trend, being up to speed with everyone else. This was about year 2000, and Botox and breast implants were sweeping this country. I did it all. I had my forehead injected several times with the nerve numbing, neurotoxin Botox. Not for a second was any part of my focus connected to health. My diet, my stress level, and the toxic medications I was swallowing every single day, were not connected to my health, not in my book. There were no health concerns from me, or from the medical system when looking at my life and lifestyle. I could not see that I had weak organs staring me in the face, and that what I was doing was going to blow up on me. I could not see that what I was eating, and had been brought up on, was getting in the way of my health. I could not see that the pills I was being fed were slowly killing my whole system from within.

Now, this blows my mind to even think about - but then, it did not even stir a mild breeze.

My hands were tingling, and my right foot was getting heavy and numb. Sometimes I felt my fingers going completely numb, and it was just as scary as it sounds. My foot felt slow. I often had to use a lot of extra effort to get it to respond to me while walking. This had been going on for a few years, and my doctor decided it was time to dig deeper. It was time for a whole hospital work-up of tests. I was sent to the neurological department at the University Hospital, to be tested for MS, multiple sclerosis. They were going to scan my brain. I remember so well the hospital corridors, the examination rooms and the tests, but I do not recall any feelings attached to the experience. I was so thrown by all the appointments and tests that weren't going anywhere, that I think I was giving up on me ever experiencing a healthy body. Whatever test I did, and whatever medication I was prescribed, it never got me well. I felt doomed, but had no choice but to keep going. They did an MRI, and also decided to do a lumbar puncture. A painful procedure, again done during lunchtime. I remember being irritated that they kept me after the spinal tap. I had meetings to go to! They keep you lying down for a few hours, as many will experience severe headaches. Lying still was not my favorite thing to do. I did better on the run. If I sat still, I could hear my heart, my breath, both uneasy. I was working this whole time, also being an aerobics instructor and spinning instructor after hours. How? I have no idea!

Well, they found nothing on the scans, and except for my reflex on the sloppy foot being weak, I was *fine*. I was relieved. I had dodged another bullet. MS, not something I saw as a future diagnosis. This was getting too serious. I knew that I never felt well, but I was not really sick, or was I?

No one likes a puffy face, and certainly not swollen eyes. Nothing feels unhealthier than looking unhealthy. During this period of my life, I usually looked pretty good. That was a great place to hide, the place of looking good and healthy. Being physically fit and apparently full of energy, with long shiny hair, puts you in the healthy place. People perceive you as the picture of health. Well it wasn't so. Not at all. Looking back on older pictures, I can see degeneration. Most people would not be able to see that, but I can see ill health surfacing. My skin was wrinkling up, and my eyelids were drooping. Anyway, I started to have swollen eyes. Under, over, around, all swollen 24/7. I was desperate. What was going on? Why was my body acting this way? No answers, and the times were a bit different than today, there was no Facebook or Internet forums. You couldn't just Google it. We were used to accepting the medical authority that we had access to, even more so than today. We were programmed to listen and do, as health was not in our own hands, the doctors were in charge.

More medication was heading my way. I was put on a heavy diuretic drug known as Furix. I loved it! It worked instantly! It took away all the puffiness, and even after a night out I could mask the look of a hangover. You see, at this time I did not tolerate alcohol very well. My hangovers became stronger, and it took longer and longer to recuperate. My liver was speaking to me.

I woke up one morning, and could not lift my right arm. Not for the life of me could I lift that arm. It was so painful to even try to lift it, there was just no way. Getting dressed for work was nearly impossible. One arm down, and my enthusiasm went with it. What the heck? My husband drove me to work that day. There was no way I could drive a car. I was in charge of rebuilding a bar, a restaurant, and the whole reception area of a hotel. Staying home was not an option. I had to do my job, people were counting on me. Pills were popped, not generating much relief, but I could do this. My left foot had started to give me some hints also, and I remember having to take off my shoes, to relieve the pain. I went shoeless during the day. My father picked me up from work, and drove me to their house. I remember this because I never had to be driven anywhere before. I felt disempowered and weak. I felt lost, and my health was starting to get in the way of my life. That is what I saw. My body was talking to me, but I saw it as getting in my way.

The doctor told me I had a frozen shoulder, and gave me a shot of cortisol right into the joint. He nailed it, but only for a little while. It froze again, and I was left with the hanging arm for months. It was the inflammation that was starting to hit my joints. My foot, my shoulder, slowly and steadily. I had no idea what the next ten years were going to hold for me, and that my experience of *Hell* had not even started.

The next part of this story was to me a very scary one. This was the first time I thought I was going to die.

I was in a meeting concerning the take-over of a local Pub and restaurant. My husband and I were going to invest in a side business. The stress level had obviously hit an all-time high, and while in this meeting my body started to fade. I got so dizzy I could not sit in my chair. I was helped to the floor, while given a piece of chocolate to eat. I remember someone saying, "She has probably not eaten anything. She hardly eats". I felt frustrated, trying to communicate that I was most definitely eating. Being fit and slim did not mean you did not eat! My husband helped me to the car, and with the seat all the way down, I could lay flat on my back. We drove home.

I was not getting any better, and after an hour or so, sitting in a recliner in our living room, I was slipping in and out of awareness. Everything was spinning, and I could not think straight. My heart was pounding. It was beating way too fast. It was hard to breathe, and I was getting scared. I felt I was going to die. I really believed this was it.

We contacted the hospital, and were told to come as soon as possible. I was reluctant, I felt faint, and all I wanted was to curl up in my own bed. Still, we were worried, so I gave in, and we were soon on our way to the emergency room. The place was packed. Beds all over the place. I was floating, and Helge was holding me up. *Hello, I can't do this!* My thought was to leave, I wanted to go home, I needed to lie down. So sick. I was soon given a bed, and was happy to be able to tilt over. The symptoms stayed the same, and the waiting went on for hours. Finally, I was given a small separate room to continue my wait. My husband left. He had the children to attend to, so I was all alone. The hours were endless. My heart was beating irregularly, and anyone who has had that experience knows how fearful it can be. I was sure this was where I would die. I was sure of it. I felt sorry for my children. They would be without a mother.

When I was finally attended to, I was examined, then moved to the observation room. They were going to monitor me overnight. I remember the doctor not liking my frozen shoulder and was mumbling that someone should look at the larger picture. Someone should look at my whole health history. His thoughts got lost in me being sent home with a diagnosis of having had an anxiety attack. It was all anxiety, and no one could know where it came from, meaning they could not say why it had hit me like that. There were no connections here, at least none that would be worth connecting it seemed. Me? Really? An anxiety attack, just like that? I had never been anxious my entire life! Well, I would experience otherwise. How little did I know...

Even now, I was so conditioned to do what was expected of me, that I worked opening-night of the new pub and restaurant with a double sided pneumonia. Arms and legs that were telling me inflammation Hell was about to show up, and me working all night. I put on my heels, my smile, and covered my fever with makeup, doing what I was used to do. Being me at my best, wearing the mask of the strong and the serving. No one twisted my arm, and no one forced me to do anything. This was all me, ignorant, lost me.

It was getting harder to teach my spinning classes every week. My left foot was now inflamed. It was impossible to wear my every-day heels, meaning impossible to wear them without being in pain, which are two completely different things. Never the less I wore them, IN pain, every day. Spinning was getting to be impossible though, as I could not get into my spinning shoes. The doctor was reluctant, but sent me to do an MRI of the foot, and the test came back with a clear message. They found arthritic changes. This changed everything, and fast. They ordered blood tests left and right. The nightmare was about to start. In the meantime, my hands were swelling, and my overall health was to the point of me having to get a sick leave. I was a full time sick-person, waiting for test results, sitting outside laboratories and in waiting rooms. They found what they had been looking for.

The diagnosis was clear. Severe sero-positive rheumatoid arthritis. The bloodwork was through the roof, and I was finally declared very sick. I was scheduled to be submitted for a two week stay at a rheumatic hospital in Haugesund, a smaller town a few hours away. Sero-positive means that they found antigens in the blood, and they could certify their finding and diagnosis. I was being submitted for a full work up, a full overview, and was leaving the following week. The red light was on, and I got the sense that these tests were showing me that I was in real trouble. This was the end of anyone wondering what was wrong with me, and everyone now knew just how sick I was. From this day I became my diagnosis. I would from now on be looked at as a medical case, someone to feel sorry for, and most importantly someone who was different and not from the same tribe.

The information was tough to take in, and it would take time for me to process. I was still not grasping that this was very serious, and was keeping my *we can fix this* attitude. My doctor had put on *the serious face* when he told me, so I knew this was not good. I remember sitting in my car after being told the news, thinking; *WOW, I bet I will get no insurance now*. I had my company to take care of, a sole proprietorship. I was concerned with money. My first thought was money. My health was not what I jumped at, but the money: what would I do about money?

This was in May 2004, and it became a very special 17th of May celebration for me. I was leaving for the hospital submission the day after this National Freedom celebration. If you have ever seen a cheerful holiday celebration, this would be it. Norwegians take their National Freedom celebration very seriously. I was watching everybody cheering and celebrating as through a fog. I was not able to use my Norwegian costume, a national costume dress, that I had worn for the past 20 years on this occasion, due to my swollen hands and feet. I remember my mother being very concerned that I could not wear the dress. My hands and feet were of less concern at the time. We are all within our own stories and perception. I was completely in a different place that day, and my mind was not present with my family at all. My foundation was giving in. I was no longer on solid ground.

It felt like I was beside myself, like I was on my way to something scary and new, and I was. I was going to find out what my body had been trying to tell me for a long time. I was going to find out just how important living in a healthy body is. I was sent to this hospital in Haugesund, and I had no idea what to expect. My life had changed, I could feel it, and I felt distant to everything around me. Life in pain was getting old, and the road ahead did not seem like a dance on roses. I felt no eagerness and enthusiasm towards the future, and it was scary. I love life, I always did, and now, I didn't know anymore.

Chapter three

The shit hits the fan!

" I am at Haugesund Sanitetsforenings Revmatisme sykehus. A very old hospital for rheumatic patients, consisting of six floors. The hospital deals with rheumatic patients like me. That is all that they do. Some are here for examinations, some are staying longer for rehabilitation, and some are here to have surgery. I notice that the surgery units fill up a large part of the hospital. These people do a lot of surgery! Maybe that is the way that they fix people like me?

I drove myself here. It was a lonely drive. My thoughts have been drifting between hope, curiosity and frustration. I have no idea what to expect, and I am not sure how long they are going to keep me here. Me and my sleepover bag, together with a book and a cellphone, are in on this together. My lap is filled with papers, a large quantity of forms and questionnaires. I am looking for a pen, noticing that it is very quiet here. Scary quiet. The reception area is behind glass, and I am the only one here. I am sitting at the end of a long hallway, leading to a number of doors. No doors are opening or closing, it feels like someone is dying, it is so quiet. Some of the chairs are unnaturally high, like a crossing *between a bar stool and a chair. The pamphlets and brochures filling the table next to me are all about how to live with a debilitating chronic disease, and how to manage a joint replacement. I am freezing. It must be lunchtime or something. It is so quiet and cold. As I am answering questions about my health, my work, do I need help, and do I need special aids, my hands are in severe pain. Next question:* Are you able to write this yourself? *Am I not expected to be able to write? They know how sick I am? Being here scares me.*

A woman walks towards me. Dressed like a doctor, she is calling my name. I feel dizzy. I never did like hospitals. We are walking past a large display of metal joints. What a cheerful way to decorate, *is my thought, as I follow this woman to her office. What would one accomplish by using joint replacements as decorations? Maybe it is the interior architect speaking, but seriously. That cannot be a good thing. I am still freezing. It is hard to walk, and I am happy to see a chair.*

"Please sit," *she says. She does not have to tell me twice. She examines me, my fingers, my toes, my knees, reads some of the forms and looks at me;* "You will have a meeting with the special aids department tomorrow. They will provide you with what you need." *She is not taking her eyes of my paperwork while she speaks. I cannot think of any special aids that I will need, but that's the least of my worries at this point. What can this woman tell me about getting well and back to work?* "What are the prognosis?" *I stutter.* "When will I be able to get back to my life?" *This is what I have come here to find out. No one has been able help me figure out what is going on in my body, and now I am relying on this woman to help me. Maybe she is the one, that can get me back to my life. She now has a diagnosis, so what is the plan?*

"You have a serious autoimmune condition and will never get well again". She says.

Unaffected, she looks at me and tells me; "You will have to be medicated for the rest of your life, and will need more aids to take care of yourself as the years go by," *she continues;* "Do NOT worry, we have great surgeons today, and a number of medications we can put you on to delay the deformation of your joints. There are some new drugs that are very promising. You are young, and you need to get on them right away!"

I am in shock. I know that I have been sent here because I need some serious fixing, but she's talking about the rest of my life? This woman in a white coat who is not looking at my face, is telling me I will never get well again. This makes me feel sick to my stomach. She is loosely telling me that she has never seen extreme blood counts like mine, and that she has never seen someone come in with such swollen hands. She calls on a nurse to give me Prednisone intravenously right away. This cannot be good. This can not be a good thing. Right away? My cells are shrinking. They are screaming at me; "No, no, no!"

"We will keep you here for two weeks. We will make sure you have everything you need before you leave. Get settled in and relax. Don't think so much. Having RA is not that bad at all, in fact, it is not much of a setback. The medication is fabulous, and the help is fantastic. Cheer up and enjoy the stay!" *The doctor tells me this word by word. I am just looking at her, thinking I will never be spinning, running, skiing or walking in my high heels, ever again. I am also thinking that something is very off with this scenario.* "Thank you, can I lie down now?" *This is what comes out of my mouth, as I struggle to get up from the chair. The woman looks at me for the first time and says:* "Sure, think of this as a vacation. Relax and enjoy your stay."

I am lying in bed later that first day, reading my book, waiting for the IV nurse to hook me up with real trouble. This is a book that will follow me for many years to come. "You Can Heal Your Life", by Louise Hay. While I am holding on to my book, I am also holding on to my inner voice that is telling me:

Something is not right. Your body can heal. I can heal, I *am* healed! *I am telling myself this over and over and over again.*

I have never seen myself as a spiritual person, even though I have always been open minded, knowing that there was more going on than I could perceive. Tears are running down my cheeks, and for the first time in a very long time I say a prayer;" Please, dear God, tell me what to do!" The tears are not only for myself, but for all those suffering like this, every single day. Those who feel sick and lost, and in a system where no one is concerned with how they are feeling, or what is going on in their lives.

She did not ask me what my life looked like, this woman. How was my diet? Did I have stress in my life? Did I have someone with me? She asked me nothing of the sort. It feels like it matters, but I am not sure, I am drained and alone. I feel very alone for the first time since I can remember.

I have heard about Prednisone, and I do not like what I have been hearing. People were getting what is labeled as a moon face, *where the whole face swells up, and makes you look unfamiliar and unhealthy. I feel overwhelmed, and I let the nurse do what she came to do. 0.5 liters of Prednisone, into my veins. I lie still, hooked up for a few hours, while I get more and more hyper inside. The inflamed fingers seem to have gotten a little bit better, but my whole body is shaking. I can't go to the toilet. My body is not giving up the urine. My kidneys cannot do their job. I need to talk to the doctor again. She does not like this, and she aborts the next round of Prednisone. My body cannot take it. I feel alone. What now? How will I get well without this medicine?*

The days are filled with reading, eating, and trying to keep myself calm. In the hallway they are serving waffles and red juice. Coffee is on display around the clock, and I notice the other patients are drinking coffee at all hours. My room has six beds, but only four are occupied. My roommates are walking from one treatment to another, all in need of special aids, and all constantly complaining about their terrible situation.

I have been given a schedule, appointments and tests. I enter the room of my 11.00 o`clock special aids appointment. I had help from a nurse this morning, getting dressed. I can't dress myself. I am told to squeeze a device, so they can read the strength of my fists. Not good news. I need a special knife, a can opener, and wrist supports. Well, I know that I cannot do certain things around the house anymore, so I am welcoming the gesture. With the wrist supports, I am told I can do laundry again, and drive my shift stick with less pain. The lovely woman that is testing me, is filling out some forms for me, so that I can get further help in my home town. I will need it. "You will need more and more help, so do not be afraid to ask for anything," *she says.* "You will get used to it. It might feel strange at first, but you will get used to having different tools and aids to get through your day." *Well, I am not much of an* ask for help *person. I am the* give help *person. I am the helper, not the one that needs anything. What will happen when the one that is usually helping and organizing needs the help? A scary thought.*

The eating part is interesting here. I have raised two children at this point, and even I, who do not at all see myself as a healthy eater, have a reaction to what is being served. The food is barely fit for a healthy person, in my view, and most certainly not for a sick one. I am no expert, not even close, but something feels very off when you are being served nothing but dairy, breads, sugars, and the likes. I can barely see any cooked vegetables. I will find out much later how hard it is to stay in a hospital when you are a healthy eater. It is next to impossible. Healthy eating and health should go together, and health and hospitals should go together.

They really do not know that food and health has a connection, that food and health go together like hand and glove. I have no idea myself, but this, all drugs and animal fats, sugars and additives, stirs a reaction *within me. This is not right. I am not heading down a healing path on this train. I just have no idea where to change tracks. I don`t know what to do differently, as strange as it might sound.*

The next appointment with the good doctor woman is not as cheerful on her part. I am now a complicated patient. "What medications are you on?" *She is still not looking at my face.*

"Vioxx, Nexium, Furix,", *I am listing them all. The first two are a go, but the Furix needs to be stopped. I do not know that Vioxx is going to be taken off the market a few years later. It has caused too many deaths by heart attacks. It seems there are a certain number of deaths that are within an acceptable range. Vioxx is an NSAID by the way, a non-steroid anti-inflammatory drug.*

I am listening to this doctor speaking, and all I hear is drugs and special aids. I am running a business, I have a life, is she not getting that? Is she not seeing my pain, my fear and my frustration? I am trying to listen. "I am adding Methotrexate and Prednisone," *she mumbles.* "Prednisone? That is the one that was causing my kidneys to go on strike! I did not pee, remember?" *I am fully alert now. I try to calm down, before I jump in with an opposition. I want to understand what is going on within my body. I need her to explain to me what she has planned, to help me get my life back.* "Please explain to me, what is the plan Doc?" *I am getting frustrated.*

"Do not worry at all. There is nothing to be alarmed about. Your kidneys are fine, and the medications do wonders for so many. You will lead a normal life."

A normal life? What about my business, my spinning and aerobics classes? What about all the joints that I just saw, the ones you use to replace the deteriorated ones, in people like me? What about the many operating wards, all the surgeons on call? I am sure they would not be here if all your patients were leading so-called "normal" lives? I am also wondering what normal is by her standards. I have an active life, I have two children to take care of, I have a social life, a hectic one. I do not have time to slow down. I am not made to be sick, I am full of life and have things to do. What kind of normal life will I be able to continue? My head is spinning. My mouth is silent but my inner voice is loud.

"I am not doing Methotrexate," *I hear myself saying.* "It cannot be a good idea to kill my cells! Methotrexate is a chemo drug, and I absolutely need my cells to be alive." *The doctor looks at me, not happy. Another doctor enters the room. I am outnumbered. I am sitting in front of two strangers of authority, telling me to do as I am told. I am crying now. Tears are streaming down my cheeks. I am not a big crier, but I am crying. In front of two strangers, at the age of 39, I am crying. I can´t believe this. I am crying and they are raising their voices at me? I am getting a lecture on their ability to medicate me, and that I better listen, or else... I need to do the chemo drug, even though it makes me nauseated and itchy all over my body. I know I am not getting anywhere, and all I say is* "ok". *I know I cannot kill my cells, I just can`t, but that will be between me, and me.*

They do not know why I am sick, and it seems it is not of much interest. Being a curious person at heart, I want to know, and I want to understand. I am now seeing the specialists, the ones that are supposed to know about health and sickness. I am finally there, and I need their expertise. I need to know why I am sick, and how I can get well. I want and need to be healthy, and I need to understand why the doctor would say I couldn't be? Now, I am to be medicated and sent home. Rather sooner than later, it seems.

I am now seen as a non-cooperative patient, and my body reacts negatively to what they are giving me. My attitude is not a good one, I need to calm down. "I have been reading about a new kind of medicine," *I say.* "It is only available for those that have tried the more common solutions first, with no satisfactory results." *I was not backing down. Doctor #1 was mostly concerned with me not making* *a scene, and not asking too many questions, while Doctor #2 said: "If I ever had to live with a chronic disease, I would have chosen RA." He is a healthy young man right now, so hypothetically speaking of course. So, he would have chosen this, would he? I cannot believe what I am hearing. I am sensing a lack of empathy, and I decide right here and now to not look for any human support or compassion. This was just another day at work. I feel like I am in the "Twilight Zone". He actually said he would have chosen this. Jeez, I am stunned. This is bullshit to me. Needless to say, it was not the best doctor`s appointment.*

As I leave the office, already not her favorite patient, I can tell - my thoughts go to the women that are my roommates. They are most definitely not living what I would call normal lives. Is that what we are going to be told; that pain and suffering, surgeries and medications are a part of a normal life? I know, I ask a lot of questions, but this one is getting to me at this point. Healthy is supposed to be normal, and that is where the focus should be. I am trusting the health authorities to know and support health.

Here I am, still in shock, watching these people, all in pain, all complaining, suffering and still trusting their doctor. Something inside me is telling me there is another way. This cannot be what we are intended to do with ourselves. This does not seem to represent healing to me. All I can see is suffering. I am back to reading my book.

I keep mostly to myself and read from now on. I am not interested in any complaining or medicine comparisons. My activity choices are a small TV room, a smoker`s room, my bed, and the outside, which is out of the question due to me not being able to walk much. The smokers room is visited many times a day, and yes, I am still a big smoker. No one thinks much of it, not even me. Smoking is a big part of my downhill spiral protocol. I am working really hard on getting to the very bottom of the ladder. I am giving it everything I have, and that is obviously a lot. I keep eating my chips, and I drink my diet coke. I am making sure that my body does not stand a chance.

I have a visitor, and I am not expecting any. A dear young friend of mine, currently living close to the hospital, comes to see me. He even brings flowers. I am feeling so blessed by this visit. Stian takes the time to check in on me, and to give me a much needed hug. It lifts my spirit and my day. (I still thank you for that.)

This whole being diagnosed and labeled is taking a toll on my mental and emotional state. I feel alone, I feel lost, and what I knew to be my future, has been turned upside down. My future looks like a black hole. Nothing to hold on to, and nothing to be sure of. I am feeling strange. The medications are making me feel low in energy. The pain in my body haunts me 24/7, and not being able to move much makes me feel like I am in prison. It makes me feel old and done. I have always been an active girl and woman. Now, I am confined to sitting and walking only the least amount of steps necessary. I am feeling deeply insecure. Not knowing my future, or being able to plan it, is devastating to me.

I am also affected by my surroundings. This is an old hospital, very old. The interior is cold and sterile, like most hospitals that I have seen, but this one tops the list. There is so much pain and suffering in these walls. People are in pain everywhere I look. There is no optimism, no hope. The doctors are cold and busy. This is my experience as I am walking slowly back to my room. Remember, all of this is my experience, as an observer, and a patient.

A nurse brings a message to my room the next morning, I have been assigned a new doctor. They will also apply for this new drug for me, right away. This is obviously big and good news. It is called Enbrel. I am trying to stay positive, I am getting the best of the best there is. I am confident that this will be as good as it gets. The drug is new on the market, very expensive, and the results are great. After all, my so called disease is incurable, or so they say. This is the best that I could hope for. I am relieved in a way. At least now I know what I am going to do. This is what is going to be my future. I am looking forward to getting my active life back, in any way possible. At this point I am not thinking about what all these drugs can do to me, not by a single thought. I am holding on to the Big Pharma theory, and the trust in man`s evolution. My main focus is getting back home to my family.

When I leave the hospital, I somehow feel lucky. Only a few get the chance to use Enbrel. It costs too much money. Only a few chosen ones get the opportunity to use the latest drug on the market. I feel even more lucky, thinking about it. Enbrel is an immune suppressant. I have read about it. That means that I must stop taking it if I get any form of infection, a cold, a flue etc. It also means that my body will not be able to create my symptoms anymore. I will make sure I cannot hear my body trying to speak to me. My body can cry out all that it wants, I will not be able to hear a single peep. I am breathing fresh air again, hoping to never return. But I would, many times.

Driving back, barely able to keep my hands on the wheel due to my pain, I am visioning a place of healing, a place for people to come to restore and rejuvenate their body. Where true health is in focus, and where the atmosphere is healing and inviting. There will be running water, calming music and the smell of flowers and herbs. Little seeds are being planted in me. There is something more than this, I just don't know what. Right now, this is what I am doing, this is all that I know."

I can do this, I must!

After a few weeks the good news came in a letter. The drug application went through! Everything would be fine now. These were self- administering shots. I was supposed to inject them twice a week, into my abdomen. I received a letter telling me that I would get an appointment at the hospital I was admitted to, to learn how to administer these shots. They did not have an appointment available for at least two months though, but as soon as they did, I would be notified. I am reading this, in severe pain, and with the prescription in my hand. This was not going to happen. I could not wait that long, no way. I called several rheumatologists, private practicing ones in my home town, and bingo! One of them felt for me, and agreed to see me the very next evening! He was going to show me how to administer the shots, and that was that. I had never used a syringe or injected anything to myself or anyone else, so this was completely new to me. Luckily this was not a complicated deal, so I was good to go. I thanked the good doctor for his help, and felt ready to get to it. Everything was happening very fast, and I was trying my best to keep my emotions out of this. The fact that I was accepting to be a chronically sick and medicated person for the rest of my life, was hard to swallow. I had not even turned 40, and I had no idea how to incorporate that scenario into my mind. I was living this, but at the same time it was like I was not. It was surreal and crazy, and I was sucked in, following the path of a chronically ill woman.

Before long the skin around the injection site was getting red and swollen. It itched, and to me it looked like hives. All normal, I was told. I had to constantly move the injection site, not to damage my tissue and form too much scar tissue. My stomach looked like the World map after a while, and I started to use my thigh instead. Oh well, at least I was walking around. It was still summertime, and to be able to move around kept me sound. I would use my camera, take pictures of nature, and I fell in love with the outdoor in a much deeper way. It was like it was calling me. The life force of nature was showing me some soothing energies.

I am a happy person by nature, the positive kind, but something was now changing. My mood was changing. I felt heavy, like everything was getting darker. I had used to be cheerful, even in challenging situations, but now I felt very different. It was like a switch had been turned off. I did not feel like myself anymore, and had to keep going on my strong willpower alone. It was like the positive outlook that was natural for me, now had to be willed by my intention and strength. I "knew" that this was not who I was, and that concerned me. Enough so that I contacted the hospital to let them know.

Depression was a common side effect of the drug, I was told, and to give them a call back if it got any worse. "I need to get used to not being happy anymore?" Their answer did not please me.

I spent a lot of time painting now, as an escape, and as a desperate wish to express myself. Painting became one of my greatest passions, and I lost myself in it. I was creating large abstract pieces on canvas, and had several exhibitions. They sold out, and I kept creating. I kept going and I kept doing. At least I was expressing myself, even if I was not listening. Getting an outlet for my creativity had been an important part of my life. I used to be a dancer, a gymnast, an interior architect, an artist and I loved to write. As a child, I was a piano player, and a fairly good one I was told. Later, I wouldn't be able to keep doing any of these things, and I would miss painting for many years to come.

The mask was harder to keep on, but still very doable. The strong woman, happy, active and positive, would be able to carry on for a while still. The body had gotten a new substance that could hide its symptoms. It was getting its fix, its medicine, twice a week. It had gotten another cold shoulder from me. I had no intention of listening. My life was going to continue as I had planned. Working, travelling, partying, exercising, and being the fix-it-all person.

I could still *look* healthy and happy, and act like it too, so I would!

Chapter Four

Denial, and resistance to change.

As the medication kicked in, my joints were slowly getting better. The swelling was going down, and I could move freely again. I was even able to wear my high heels now, and I could not have been happier. Did I mention that I am a shoe freak? I've always loved shoes, and I own many. It had been such a loss for me, to not be able to wear my beautiful shoes. They make the entire outfit, don`t they?

Anyway, I was back to wearing my heels, working and running. Yes, I was even back to running, and boy did I enjoy it! I was taking long walks with my husband, and really enjoying being back in nature. I still brought my camera, and found so much joy in taking pictures on my daily walks. Being active was my thing, and how I felt free and recharged. My life started to look and feel like it should again. It was back to where it was before everything became unbearable. I was able to resume my schedule, or close to it, yet something just wasn't the same. A dark cloud was hanging over me, and a strange new feeling was arising from within.

Something *was* very off. I was getting more and more fatigued as the days passed. My energy levels had dropped big time. The happy-feeling-better period was over. My stomach really acted up again, and I was getting a sense of inner uneasiness. My intuition was trying to get my attention. I felt an inner turbulence. My inner knowing was not happy about this situation, my medications and my living habits.

For a while I could deal with all of this, the pain and the low energy. I was doing my best to keep my business, and I was travelling, bringing my Enbrel and my other medications with me. The Enbrel had to be carried in a cooler to not lose its potency. It came with me on several cruises and skiing vacations. I remember noticing new symptoms little by little, but I was keeping up appearances the best that I could. My body would react to room temperature water - as if it was steaming hot. I could no longer tolerate any heat, so being in the Caribbean was torture. I used to love the heat! Now, all it did was make me sick, anxious and fatigued. Any form of stress would make my joints swell again, and that meant I would need to take more Prednisone. I was told by the doctor to take as many pills as I needed on my vacation, no limits at all. It was about living life, he said. I deserved it, so just pop those pills! I did.

The spiral was going downward, and I was hanging on by a thread. I was hanging on by less than a thread. I was holding on to everything that felt like my normal self, even if it was pure terror. This is a human trait I have been studying a lot over the later years. How we tend to hold on to what is, even if it is killing us. Even if what we are doing is hurting us, we would rather keep doing it than change. I was afraid of losing everything that I believed defined me. My job, my looks, my friends and my social status. I was scared to death of losing what was killing me, of losing what was hurting me. I was at war with my own body. I was so disconnected from myself, I could not find a way to see the simple truth. It was staring me in the eye, and I could and would not see it. Not yet.

Over the next two years I was getting worse and worse. Yes, you heard me, *two years*! Unbelievable, right? I was getting more and more anxious. This was very new to me, feeling so uneasy and jumpy. I had experienced that one incident several years prior, but now I was being consumed by uneasiness. I did not have a steady heartbeat. My heart was skipping beats. It felt like it was stopping, and then restarting. I learned that this is referred to as missed beats. Well, to me it did not matter, my heart was not happy, and neither was I. The heart is a vital organ, and I knew very well that it needed to beat, preferably at a steady rhythm. Sometimes it would race for a while, and sometimes it felt like it would stop all together. It felt like game over. What a constant reminder of not being healthy, and what a constant reminder of how easily life could end. On top of this, I felt like I was having the flue constantly.

Knock, knock, is anybody home in this body? Where is the Head of operations? Who is in charge? It was time to visit my regular doctor again, reluctantly.

This same doctor stayed with me for 25 years. He had been prescribing all my drugs and scheduled all of my specialist appointments. Still, I saw that with this serious RA diagnosis, he felt I was now out of his territory. This was out of his league. I was back in his office, but as long as I had RA written all over my forehead, all my symptoms needed to be checked by a rheumatologist.

My rheumatologist was still a few hours away, in Haugesund, and it took me months to get an appointment. In the meantime, all I could do was wait. I would be notified, and here is the crazy part; I finally get an appointment with the rheumatologist, and I drive myself to Haugesund with a heart that is skipping beats and all. I feel like shit, literally. I sit down with the doctor, tell him all my symptoms, and he looks at me and says: *"I am only interested in your joint's health. These other symptoms you'll have to talk to your regular doctor about."* I am staring at this man. *"But I believe they could be side effects of my medicine. It has gotten worse and worse since starting Enbrel. My joints are ok, but my insides are falling apart,"* I tell him.

No, that was not an interesting or important observation. Nothing of what I was experiencing had anything to do with the medication. There was no connection what so ever. *"Just keep on doing what you are doing and go see your regular doctor if you are not feeling well,"* is what I get in return for driving all day to see him. I am silently shaking my head now. I am not sure how to process this. What a crazy world.

It was a long drive back, I felt lost, alone and ignored. I have value, I know this, and something has to give. I was getting nowhere.

I have no idea how many times I went to my doctor with complaints like this. I had stopped working at this time. I could no longer keep it together. The anxiety was taking over. I was constantly nauseated and dizzy, and my stomach was in great pain. I was so sick, my husband almost had to carry me to see the doctor. I could hardly sit up straight. I kept being sent home, told that I had to go to Haugesund as I had rheumatoid arthritis and I was their responsibility. I felt powerless. I was too sick to do anything, let alone travel, and I was too weak to argue.

Something was very, very off. My intuition was trying to get through to me, but still I had no idea what to do. I had a calling, and it was whispering to me.

I had bad days, and I had days from Hell. It became normal, and I was surviving by trying to find a way out. It resulted in me attending several workshops on healing and intuition. I became a Reiki healer, and my interest for healing and the spiritual aspect of life was shining through. I was searching for something new, for something that would show me the way. I had a longing for a new path, but I was locked in my own invisible prison. The prison of my mind and my programming. Much later, I would see that the weekend workshop by Brandon Bays, "The Journey", had started me on a lifesaving journey of my own. The first step had been taken, and the intention was set. Seeds had been planted, and my calling had been received. Something had shifted, I had seen my own inner power. The workshop included meditation and emotional healing work.

I remember thinking I was too young to live like this, as if it was ok at any age. I was only 41 now, and the number of things on my to-do list were many and colorful. I had never, not even for a minute, thought that there would be a time limit on my list. And what about my children? They were young, they needed their mum. Luckily they were not babies anymore. They were eighteen and fifteen years old at this time, and their support was invaluable. This is one of the largest blessings looking back, that they were not toddlers or babies. There is no way I could have taken care of them in the condition that I was in. Instead I have been blessed to have witnessed them bloom and grow into wonderful, compassionate adult human beings. Their school of life has taught them empathy and love, and for that I thank God.

Life goes on, and my little family is trying to make sense of our every-day life. Trying to hold on to the structure and meaning. Summer comes, and vacation time is up like every other summer. My husband and I have always been big fans of Tour de France. Since I was not up for airports or stressful plane rides anymore, we decided to take a road trip to France. I knew from my heart that this was not a good idea, but my will to experience got in the way. I had gotten the sense of how sick I really was, and my inner voice was yelling at me at this point. Still, the old programming that was telling me that I needed to go on a vacation, won. I was going to have a normal life, and that was that.

We drove all night, and I had to have the car seat all the way back in a lie-down position. Driving through Germany was a nightmare. Every time we stopped to use the restroom, I had to stand outside in line. The temperature was close to 100 degrees Fahrenheit. I was ready to faint, and my heart was beating off the charts. When I washed my hands in cold water, I felt they were being scalded. My nervous system was breaking down. We travelled with a tent, and my husband set up camp just off the motorway. Everything felt like it was in an emergency-mode. We needed some rest. The tent was up, and I crawled onto the little mattress. I was on my back, and Helge was concerned. Could he leave me here? He needed to get some food, and I was telling him to go. He was gone for what seemed like forever (close to 45 minutes). During that time, it was like my body was going into a state of shock. The stress, the fear, the symptoms, I was shaking and crying. He came back to find me close to hysterical, totally freaked out and falling apart. My whole system felt like it was shutting down. I was losing it. After a restless night, we packed our gear and headed back North. Game over.

I was desperate now. I called the hospital in Haugesund and was able to speak to a nurse, thank God. She said to stop the Enbrel right away. I was NOT supposed to keep taking it while having flu-like symptoms. I knew that, but in my mind this was nothing like a flu, or a cold. The nurse tells me that my body is obviously in a crisis, and that it sounded like I had an infection of some sort. I stopped my medications that very day.

What would happen to my joints now? I was still able to move around fairly well, and remembered vividly how easily that could change. I was concerned, I did NOT want to go back to immobility and severe pain. I had no choice, and to be honest, my intuition was starting to get to me. It was telling me that what I was doing was killing me, that I needed to wake up and listen. Instead the shit hits the fan again, and I am heading for another crash.

"I cannot stand up straight, I am continuously fainting. We are on our way to the ER. I am afraid. This is not good. My husband is helping me inside. I can barely walk. The woman that meets us, makes sure that I get a bed to lie on immediately. My face is pale, I am cold, and my hands are sweaty. I am nervous. I have been here before. The memories are not inviting, and I am not ready for another stay at this hospital. After returning from our so-called trip, I could no longer function. I felt like I was about to shut-down.

The doctor takes one look at me, puts his flash light on my eyes, and admits me to the cardiovascular department for monitoring. I do not remember much of how I got there, but the night is calm and uneventful. I am given my own room, and the staff are like angels. It is like I have died and gone to heaven. I am treated like a queen. They see me, smile, and feel like real compassionate people. What a true blessing, and unexpected experience. I am hopeful now. I am sure that these wonderful people will find out what is wrong with me, and help me. I am at Stavanger University Hospital, and they will know what to do."

The next two weeks turned out to be a nightmare, a never ending series of tests and examinations. A time of loneliness was ahead.

"After spending a few days on the fifth floor, or in heaven, I am now being transferred to the department of internal medicine. There are no beds available, meaning none that have a room to go with it. I am placed in the hallway. For hours I lie here, people walking by, talking and running everywhere. The sounds, the noise, the stress, the smell, and the people running to and from is getting to be too much. I am crying now. I feel lost. I am so sick, I feel terrible, and I just lie here. I am watching an old man get his diapers changed while in the hallway. Where am I? What is this place? No one seems to notice me, and I

haven`t gotten any instructions. No one is telling me what's going on. How long am I here for, what are they doing, and when will I get a room?

I remember that I have a cell phone with me. It's in my purse. I desperately call my husband at work. I can´t stop crying. "Please get me out of here". The poor man is there within 30 minutes, during working hours, concerned for his wife. I can rest. A friendly face is here. I feel weak and broken. As I am lying here, what kind of wife am I? These are the thoughts that run through my head. I have been the one taking care of me and my family my whole adult life. I am the fixer and the strong one. This is tearing me apart, feeling so helpless and weak. Crying, desperate, feeling like my body is dying on me. This is not me!

I am placed in a small room the next morning. A tiny room with four beds, and this will be my home for the next two weeks. I am staring at the ceiling, listening to my heartbeat. It is not beating right, and I try to focus on thinking good thoughts. I close my eyes and listen to my breath. Someone calls my name, and I open my eyes. A young nurse is standing by my bed. "There is a number of tests scheduled for you," she says. "A doctor will come by later this week, but for now, just stay ready for testing. Someone will come for you." She tells me that I am being booked for a whole series of tests. They are doing the works; Blood tests, stool test, gastroscopy, colonoscopy, an ultrasound of my heart, and an MRI of my head. I will be evaluated by a neurologist and a rheumatologist. My symptoms are of great concern, and they will make sure they test everything. I look at the nurse telling me this. She looks at me with a sad face. She is feeling sorry for me. I can see it in her eyes. Please do not feel sorry for me, I will be fine.

These tests are really taking a toll on me. There was no energy in my account, nothing, and I am drained to the core by all of this. I am wheeled to all of my tests and appointments, in my bed. It is the easiest way. I feel like I am in a sick-factory. Wheeled here and there with my chart on my chest. No one looks at my face, only at my chart. Left in hallways, being delivered and picked up again. No doctors to talk to, no nurses, only tests and assistants. The hours in bed are long, only disturbed by the daily visits from Helge, and a few from my children. I am fine by myself, by all means, but the time is mostly spent waiting. On some days there's absolutely nothing going on, no tests, not a single thing. My lesson on patience has started, and a hard lesson it is.

Food is served three times a day, and typically includes some loaf of bread, eggs, cheese, potatoes, gravy and fish or meat. I am not that fond of food. It is not my passion. The bread and red juice, the potatoes with meat, is not at all helping my digestion. Still, I keep eating what I am served, watered down with my very own diet coke. During the last few years, I cannot hold down much food. I feel full even when not eating. My digestion has had enough, and food is not my friend.

It is the second week, and I am on leave for the night. I drive myself home with my upper body packed with little stickers and cables. I have no idea how I was able to drive, but I was, I did. My heart is being monitored. I have to sleep with these things, and drive back the next morning. I feel overwhelmed. I have always taken care of myself, but I am sensing someone else should take over, if only for a little bit. I am sensing it is time to lie down and let everything else be. As I am focusing on the road, driving my new red convertible, this is what is dawning on me. I should not be driving, and someone should be taking the wheel, right now. This is madness. My whole way of living is madness! This is me, it is summer, I am young, happy and active. I am living beside myself, like in a bubble. My life seems unreal, as I sense this alarming feeling of something being completely off.

"You are right; your heart is not beating regularly." *The doctor looks at me.* "I know, I told you that!" *I am so tired of this.* "Your heart looks fine though, so just take some magnesium, and I am sure you will be good." "Ok doc, thanks." *That is really all I want to say. Thank you, thank you. I am happy about the news, truly - I am - even though I am not confident about the solution.*

I am waiting again, this time for the rheumatologist to write up and sign the papers that will set me free. I want out. I am worn out, and I am ready for my own bed. I need to rest now. I need to figure out what to do next. After me sitting on a chair in a hallway for four hours, he shows up. I am following him slowly to his office down the hall. I am shaking. I am eager to hear what is wrong with me - besides the obvious. My joints are not working. He tells me something I am not prepared to hear: "We found nothing. Get back on Enbrel, we do not believe it can cause these symptoms."

I just look at him. I know when this started, and I know how my symptoms and this whole nightmare has evolved while on that medication. I know that something is seriously wrong. I know that my body is shutting down, and this doctor is telling me to never mind? All I say is: "Ok, thank you."

That`s it. I feel numb.

What about the Lyme connection, I wonder. I remember that doctor bringing up the topic earlier. It was not the first time I had heard the word Lyme, but I had never given it much thought. I really do have all the symptoms to go with it, and I could see why he would think in that direction. He continues to tell me that even though my symptoms would fit perfectly, there is no way of testing it at this stage. It is most likely a chronic late stage. All they can offer are years of antibiotics, so I better forget all about it, and get back on the Enbrel before my joints deteriorate. There would be no point in me being diagnosed with Lyme disease, as they would not be able to help me with that. The medications I were on, would not be a good match for a Lyme diagnosis. The Doctor looks at me and says: "If you have Lyme, we could not give you the Enbrel, it would not be a good match. We would not be able to suppress your immune system if you were battling a spirochete like Borrelia. Please just focus on your RA, on saving your joints. Move on, and live your life." Ok, I get it, I am screwed. If I'm experiencing Lyme, the Enbrel will kill me, and if I am not, *it can kill me anyway. If I stop, my joints will get crippled and leave me handicapped, so, I am screwed."*

I was one step closer to hitting rock bottom. There were no solutions here, none which I could live with. I dragged myself out of there, making a deal with myself. This was my absolute last hospital visit. This was it. I was not going back, no matter what!

Out of fear of losing my joints I started back on Enbrel the next week. I felt lost, and was desperately trying to hold on to something that would save me from losing everything I knew and loved. I needed to be able to walk on my feet. For more than fifteen years I had been in business as an interior architect. I had been the aerobics and spinning instructor, and I had loved it! Now, I had to give up my business, I could no longer do any work out and training, and I was scared into taking these shots.

I was an expert at rebuilding and creating restaurants and bars, working for the major hotels and restaurants in my part of Norway. I did everything from the blueprints, the drafts, the ordering of inventory, the follow ups and the physical project management. I had a fantastic office space. It took me a long time to build and model it, and to let that all go, was hard on many different levels. I remember sitting in my lounge, looking at the space I had created. It was a tear filled process. Looking back at all the meetings that had taken place here, and all the people I had met. My work was present all over town, and even going out for dinner would hurt for a long time. It was my identity at the time. I was Hilde, the interior architect. I was the one to call if you needed to get anything fitted or built for your hotel or restaurant. Now it was all gone. My health would not let me continue. I sold off most of the inventory, and hung on to my office furniture and a few other things. They had sentimental value. My office desk was given to me by my first mentor when I was very young. A ship owner who had let me grow and learn, designing cruise ships back in the '80-s. The furniture is still in my home.

So, I started yet another course of Enbrel, and I am now called to visit my doctor. We are going through the papers sent to him by the hospital. The stay had produced no answers, and the conclusion was not solid. I was not in the best of moods, and I jumped when my doc was saying: *"Maybe we should send you to a psychiatric evaluation."* What? Was he telling me that I was imagining this? That I was throwing up, fainting, having a low grade fever and pains, all in my head? Would a psychiatrist fix my joints, my nausea, my stomach pains, my dizziness and my fatigue? He knew me better than this, I just stared at him. *"Are you serious?"*, I said. My mood was not getting any better. Just what I needed, less support.

"I know," he says, *"I just don't know what to do with you. I cannot bare to see you like this, but I have no idea what to do with you!"*

During this time, I had been receiving money from the government, a prolonged sick leave from not being able to work. I was working together with a great woman in the system of NAV, The Norwegian Labor and Welfare administration. Together we made a plan for me, on how I could keep going, and be able to create a new life with less stress.

I was still in the creating mode you see, and was going to keep doing as much as this body was able to handle, or not handle. I took up studying for one year, revisited some old subjects, and polished some old grades. Then, I applied to the University. I was going to study journalism. Yes, I was! I loved to write, and I was going to drown myself in work again.

I was going to keep going, and to keep avoiding the elephant in the room.

My hard work that year paid off. My wish was granted and I was accepted by the University. My ego felt amazing. I was one of the privileged few that would join the class of 2006.

Never mind that I was throwing up between lectures.

Never mind that the anxiety was so strong, I could hardly sit through a whole session. Never mind that I was in constant pain.

Never mind that I was flat on my back every day after classes, and that I stayed like that until the next day.

Never mind that I was totally exhausted.

My reflexologist at the time was telling me that I had a total adrenal burn out. There was nothing left. My adrenals, my kidneys, were totally slapped. My strong genes had kept me going, but she tried to explain to me that I was heading for a fall, I needed to slow down.

The Enbrel was still with me, the Prednisone, the painkillers, Vioxx, the Nexium and the Somadril. Quite a cocktail. What they all were, is not important. What they were helping me achieve, I would soon find out.

You see, together, they had been the overload this sick body did not need. In the midst of its cry for help, it was getting slapped down, until it could take no more. I was fighting the inevitable with my whole life-force. All my power went into the resistance of change and the resistance of awakening. I was using all my strength to not listen, and I was strong.

I needed a break. I knew my time at the University was going to be short lived. I knew I could not continue with what I was doing. I knew I had to change *big time*, but how? My husband and I decided to take a weekend trip to Barcelona, to try to get away from everything. As if I could get away from *me*! I remember I so wanted to be able to feel happy and healthy. I had only one wish at this time, and that was to be able to wake up and not feel pain. To be able to live for just one day, without the discomfort and the despair that I was experiencing.

The trip was the furthest from fulfilling those wishes imaginable. I spent ours in the hotel bed in pain, and I had to realize, this was not me anymore. I was done travelling, and I was done having fun. I was done.

The night we arrived home after our trip, I had the dream that changed everything.

I had an experience that changed the course of my whole life. This dream was the first of many guiding dreams and messages. It was *the* turning point. One single dream or vision, would wake me up to change the course of my life. It was time.

"I am looking at this enormous barrel, the metal kind that some use for burning garden leaves. I remember it being red, and all my needles, all the syringes, are in that barrel. They are sticking up, every shot I ever did, all put into that one barrel. It is filled to the rind! I keep staring at it as it explodes. The whole thing blows up, and I wake up in a state of shock! It was scary real, I could smell the fire, the smoke."

That whole day I felt overwhelmed. I kept throwing up between classes, but it was like it didn`t matter anymore. Nothing mattered. Not me, not what I was doing, not my body, and not my life. I drove home early. I laid down on the living room sofa, and that was that. I just laid there. I was done. This was it. I had made up my mind. This had to stop, right now, right this very minute. I was done.

No more.
No more anything.

No more feeling like I was going to die, not knowing how to get help.

No more medications that only kept making me worse.

No more doing what I did not want to do.

No more acting like I was fine, when I was not.

No more trying to look great, when I felt like crap.

No more being afraid of anything.

No more NOT listening to ME and my body.

No more bullshit.

I was done!

My husband found me on the sofa after work. I was still lying in the same position. When I sat up, this is what I told him:

"I am lying down now, and I will lie here until one of two things happen; Either I get healthy, or I die. I do not care which, as long as it is one of them. No more medications, I AM DONE! This, I cannot do anymore. This is not living. I am done!"

At 42, my body did not want to keep signaling me anymore. My whole being went on strike to save my life. I had been called. Change had happened.

Even though everything is constantly changing, we seem to be resistant of change itself. We have the power to change our lives, yet we most often do not want to own that power. To recognize it, to look truth in the face and to realize that we are capable of change, is hard. It is sometimes way out of reach for us, to believe in our self-creative powers. It seems we would rather stay miserable than change. Change, even though it would make our life better, is a scary thing. We find some sort of comfort in the known, and hold on to it, even though it is hurting us.

I was no different, and was clinging to my lifestyle and beliefs for my dear life, although it was slowly killing me.

I had spent my whole adult life building. I was building a family, a business, relationships and status. Oh yes, I was building the stereotype life, picket fence and all. The good girl syndrome was really keeping me on track. When my body would not follow me anymore, not even unwillingly, it was almost like a shock to me. I had always been able to "man" up, so to speak. To put on a happy face and do what I believed was needed of me, no matter what. I had always been able to look my best, and to be the helping, fast track, fix-everything girl that people could rely on. Well, something was about to change, big time.

The fear of change is overwhelming for most of us. To break free from old programming and conditioning is hard, and it takes courage and strength.

I believe that we all have that courage and inner strength that it takes to turn around any given situation. I believe that we all have the ability to break free and to take charge of our own lives. The fear of change is an illusion that is holding us back from experiencing our true potential. We are strong enough to change everything. We all have so much potential, and our body is always on our side. I was going to trust my body from now on. I was going to trust myself, and my intuition. I was going to trust God and the creation. I was going to CHANGE something!

Progress is a choice, a commitment to self. I had not only been medicated with chemical drugs prescribed by a doctor. I had been self-medicating with cigarettes, alcohol, foods, caffeine and much more. I had been running away from the real issue, *me*. I was the one creating this, and only I could un-create it, I knew that. How? I had no idea, and if I was wrong, so be it. I was ready to find out. We use all these substances to run from our feelings, our lives and our emotions. I was done running; I had caught up with myself.

The fear of change is an illusion that is holding us back from experiencing our true potential.

My feelings were all over the place. I felt a sense of freedom, yet a total feeling of being left alone and without any path to follow. My mind was empty and my body was tired. I was done, and yet I was ready. I kept saying these words over and over again in my head:

"Dear God, please help me. Show me the way to health, please show me the way. I am ready for complete healing. I am ready."

NOTE: *As a reference, taken from the RX list, some of the side effects listed on the Enbrel medications are:*
Pain in the stomach, fever, night sweats, severe nausea, loss of appetite, depression, generalized pain, weight loss, feeling full after eating a small amount, feeling of illness, weakness, feeling sad and empty, chills, sore throat, flu symptoms, heartburn or indigestion, tiredness, inability to move arms or legs, irregular heartbeat, chest pain, swelling, changes in mood, fast heartbeat, numbness, burning pain, joint pain or swelling, swollen glands, headache, heart failure, loss of consciousness, troubles sleeping, seizure, black bloody stools, eye pain, rashes, lymphoma, leukemia, anemia, and many more.

This is to show that many of my symptoms and my deterioration was obviously greatly affected by my drug intake. Any chemical is a great burden to the human organism, as it is acidifying and toxic.

PART TWO

THE NAKED TRUTH.

Chapter Five

Desperation and confusion.

W hen you stop all medications, the body will show you how sick you really are. I thought the shit had hit the fan, so to speak. It had not, not yet.

My body was about to show me some real truth. After masking my symptoms for years, I was terrified of finding out the state of health that I was *really* in. I had cancelled every social appointment, I cleared my calendar completely. No more going to events feeling like crap. No more wearing the mask, yet dying within. I had been to so many parties and events, while all I wanted to do was to be home, by myself, in bed. I longed for those soft covers. Done with that! I was so fed up with feeling like I was swimming towards the current, I just wanted it all to stop. It was never about me wanting to die, it was me not wanting to live in this body anymore, not like this. It was about me not wanting to listen to another doctor telling me I would never get well. It was about me not wanting to take one single shot of Enbrel again, EVER. This was about *me*, and only about what I wanted and needed. I was done trying to fit a diseased body into an active, so-called healthy lifestyle.

I told my family, I am not doing this anymore. I told my parents and my sisters that I was really sick now, and that I was going to find a way out of this perceived Hell. I had no idea that Hell had not even begun yet, and I had no idea that my life would never be the same again, ever. I thought I was ready to handle what was coming, but I had no idea how sick I was at that time. I was used to having what I called a non-stop-hangover. I was used to being constantly nauseated and with a headache. I was used to feeling like I had a fever, aching all over, and I was getting used to not being able to move without pain. The anxiety had become a well-known companion. I was constantly uneasy. Being among people had gotten harder, and my heart was not beating regularly. It was constantly skipping beats, which made me very aware that it could stop. That alone will make you anxious, believe me. I had the hangover, I just missed the party. What a bummer.

The body was giving me a head start. It takes a few months for all the drugs to leave your system. During this time, I was going downhill very steadily. My joints could not be compared to how they were before I started the medical treatment. I had not gotten better while on this wonder drug, I had gotten *worse,* much worse. Now, exposing the naked truth, letting the body show me how it was really doing, wow, I was told a different story. I was shown first hand that what I had been doing was simply masking the symptoms, and not at all letting the body heal. Not that I was ever promised any healing, I was not. Sadly, healing was never on the agenda.

At this point, my hands can no longer make a fist, and my knees cannot bend. My feet are so swollen I cannot wear regular shoes. I can hardly bend my elbows, let alone stretch them fully to make a straight arm. My ankles are swollen and I cannot lift my arms due to my very inflamed shoulders. Every week I was getting worse. Every week without medications was a step down the stairway to what I perceived as HELL.

Still, I had made my decision. I was going to make it or break it. I was going to get well, or I was going to die trying. That was it. That was all that I knew.

I got my very first laptop, a Mac Book, and it was going to be my best friend for many years. There was no Facebook, but there was the Internet. I was reading about the Arthritis Trust, an American organization that were helping people find solutions to their arthritic problems. Oh yes, I was still labeling my so-called disease at this time. Owning my RA diagnosis. I was continuing full force, from the conventional treatments, to the non-conventional ones. I was still very much conditioned to believe that this was an actual disease, and that my body was attacking itself. That being said, it never rang true with me that my body is able to attack itself. My gut feeling always reacted when my doctor was telling me that. I mean, how is that even possible? Why would my body want to do that, ever? It took me several years to own my intuition, and to fearlessly walk the path towards Inspired. Still, I never really believed that my body and I were not on the same team. I knew that I was a part of something much larger than my body, and that health was natural. I always felt that if one was born healthy, one could be healthy again. Now I know how true that is, and beyond!

Back to the Arthritis Trust. They were convinced that RA and other so-called autoimmune diseases were triggered by a parasite, a microbe. I had one thing on my plate at that time, and only one, and that was to get my life back. This new idea grew on me the more I read about it, so I decided I was going for the kill. I was doctoring myself, using my regular doctor to write my prescriptions. Flagyl became my next chemically made pill. A strong antifungal, and a kidney terror waiting to happen. Being strong is not always working *for* you, it can also hurt you. The very same force that was driving my will to get well, was also allowing me to be careless and bold. I was fearless, without any conception of what kind of substances I was playing with. All I knew was what I read, and this drug was told to kill off these critters. I was desperate, so I loaded up on the medication. My body was invaded with mega doses to kill off whatever was keeping me sick. Bless the good doctor that prescribed them to me. I was not an easy person to turn down. I was on a mission.

The reactions were devastating. I was left bedridden with both feet swollen from my knees down. I could hardly see my ankles. The anxiety got to the point where I could no longer leave my bed. I was struggling to breathe. I remember crying out that I did not want to live anymore. I was completely drowning. My urine turned dark brown, and I hardly peed at all. I was ready to explode. I could not move my joints, and I stopped leaving the second floor of our home.

That was when my desperation showed itself in many ways. My soul was trying to tell me something, but my strength, my intellect and my will were locking me into place. I was going to *fix* this. I was going to go after what was making my joints go downhill. My body was deteriorating and degenerating fast, and I had no idea where to start. After my Flagyl experience, I decided I would stop going to any doctor's office. This had to stop, me doing the pill thing. There was no more strength, and I was getting to the point where only seeing a waiting room would make me want to throw up.

I made my upstairs room my fort. I had my day bed, a TV, my computer and my determination.

I could manage the few steps to the bathroom still, but I did not go down the stairs. My husband left me food by the day bed every morning, before he went to work. My days were now consisting of eating, sleeping and searching for health on my laptop. That was it, period. On some days I would read for hours, and others, only for a little while. All depending on how I was feeling, and if I had any energy.

I kept searching, and I finally found a doctor who was open to alternative approaches. He was in Oslo, but since I was not up for travelling, he agreed to consult me via telephone. This was before Skype. I went from my regular doctor's care to his care, and what a ride that was! First of all, he diagnosed me with Lyme disease, chronic, late stage. That means, that my tick-bite back in '94 might have been the tipping point for my toxic overloaded body. Who knows, the important part for me at this time was to be seen, heard, and taken seriously. He needed blood tests, a true nightmare for me. Now I had to go back to the doctor's office after all. Taking blood from someone who cannot stretch their elbow is not easy. Getting the blood out of me, was a real struggle. It felt like I was in a war zone, trying to survive. This was the last time I went, after that, no more.

My new alternative-friendly doctor did not like my blood test at all. They showed that I was very inflamed all over my body. I was systemically inflamed. My kidneys were struggling, and so was my liver. I was severely anemic, and he did not at all like me not having closer supervision. Luckily he agreed on calling me every week and to help me the best that he could. He ordered stool test kits and food intolerance kits. This was an effective distant doctor-patient relationship. The stool test came back with alarming results. I had an overgrowth of several not so good bacteria in my intestines. The test was positive for Giardia, and it showed severe Klebsiella pneumonia overgrowth. There were more, but those are all I can recall. My new doctor got so concerned with the results, that he put me on Cipro, the antibiotic that will kill anything and burden your kidneys until they cry. Remember the one that I was put on for my H-Pylori infection in my stomach? That one, and my kidneys cried. After that, my knees started to swell. My lymphatic system was becoming seriously stagnant, and I could say good bye to walking anywhere soon. My knees were so huge, they could definitely not be bent, and going to the bathroom became an almost impossible task. You could hear me getting up, walking and sitting down on the toilet, moaning the whole time.

The food intolerance test came back positive for more foods than I can even remember. I was never 100% sure of those tests. I did several during the years, but I was never 'all in' with the results. The insecurity grew when they all came back with different findings. I had no clue about diet at this point. I was doing my best to eliminate things that I read could trigger any inflammation in the body. I was moving away from the processed sugar, but remember, I was still a smoker, a meat eater, and a processed food eater.

My jaw also got inflamed, and I could no longer open my mouth. I could not get dressed by myself, so I wore a robe during the day. I was trying to make day and night different, so I made little rituals like these; Day - robe, night - no robe. Day - Therese's old bed, night - my own bed.

This was my all-time low. I could barely get one finger into my mouth, and I could not get up from anywhere by myself. I was desperate, and I was holding on to the one shining star I could find at the time, Louise Hays. She is the author of "You can heal your life", and was also my main motivator for a long time. I had held on to that book since I was in the hospital in Haugesund, and it was barely in one piece now. Together with Doreen Virtues meditations, I was reading her books and listening to her meditations several times a day. Louise's affirmation CD's were constantly playing in my room. It was my background "music". Her voice still calms my cells, and I never get tired of listening to this woman. So gentle and so positive, such a great inspiration. Her way of speaking and reading is so easy to understand, such a simple message told beautifully. I was not at all used to meditating or stilling my mind, and her step by step guidance was a lifesaver.

The worst that could happen to me at this time, was being left alone. My husband went on several business trips, and also on a vacation trip while I was bedridden. Those were the hardest times. Being alone. When you feel like you are dying is when you really connect with your darkest side. I had to feed myself, which took every little bit of energy that I could find, and I was constantly afraid I would die. Well, maybe I was not literally afraid of dying, as much as I was afraid of being taken to the hospital. I was afraid of there being a fuzz, of the ambulance having to come, and about people seeing how sick I was. I remember telling Helge before going to sleep at night. *"No matter what happens, promise me one thing. No hospitals. I would rather die than go back to the hospital."*

I was too sick to miss much of my regular life. I was disconnected with the world. I did not miss any of it, it seemed too distant. The family barely came to see me, and when they did, they would sit downstairs in the living room. Of course our friends stopped inviting us to events, and none of them came knocking at our door. Therese had left for America to work at the Epcot Center in Florida, and I was happy she didn`t have to see me like this. I was grateful that she wouldn`t see how sick and helpless I was. Thomas was still living at home, and my biggest regret was not being able to see him play soccer anymore. The amazing soul that he is, he kept growing through this whole experience. Being an old soul, his empathy and giving personality has never stopped fueling me.

Now, everything became silent. My phone had stopped ringing, and I was in this bubble of pain and loneliness. Reading on the Internet, praying, crying and raging. I was feeling all the emotions, all the anger. I was feeling hopeless and helpless. I felt I was going nowhere, and I was questioning everything. I no longer believed in the medical doctors and their training. I no longer had any hope of recovery. According to the ones that I had put my faith in, there was nothing that could be done for me. I was on my own. What did that mean really? Was there anything that I could do that *they* could not? Were they not on top of every single solution or option out there? Was that not their job?

"Dear God, please help me. Show me the way to health, please show me the way. I am ready for complete healing. I am ready."

I experienced what I perceived as a depression. Being naturally cheerful, I was not expecting this. Physical pain I could deal with. It was what I knew. This devastating despair was new to me, and it was tearing me apart. It was like all the lights went out, and all meaning disappeared. It was not apathy, more like a deep soul cry, and a release of everything that was connected to my ego, myself, and my dreams for the future.

I wanted to die, I wanted to be released from my earthly expectations and life. I wanted to move on, to set myself free. I felt trapped, and I wanted to fly. I cried a lot during this period. Cried for my pain, but also for the whole world. I was crying for all of us that were suffering at the time.

What can I do?
Why am I here?
What kind of life will this be in the future?
How can I save my life?
Why am I alive?

At night, before going to sleep, I used to ask God to take me home. The thought of another day in this body was too much. All I wanted was out, I wanted to go home, and to feel free.

Life became very dark, and my soul cried as I was getting ready to let this all go.

Then I died.

The dark night of the soul.

After my intense experience with the Dark Night, I came across a lot of information on the topic. It is a well known term in spiritual and Christian literature, and my heart was opened by reading about the phenomena that I had known nothing about. As I kept reading, I felt more and more at peace.

Many believe they have done something wrong when the symptoms of the *Dark Night* appear. It is normal to think that something is wrong with us, that we are losing our minds. We feel as if we are stuck in the dark, and that we will never see the light again. We feel completely alone. We keep looking for the light, as we are used to running away from the dark. This time we cannot run, it is not possible. It totally swallows us.

The pain we feel is the pain we have tried to suppress for years, decades, and previous lifetimes even. It is now finally coming to the surface to be healed. I had been praying for complete healing, and little did I know that this experience was going to be a big part of it.

The term goes back a very long time, always used to describe the collapse of the perceived meaning of life. The feeling of complete meaninglessness and loss of self. In the modern world we might confuse this experience with what we call depression, but it is not. There is no meaning to anything, and everything feels meaningless. The dark night can be triggered by an event in your life. You might lose your job, someone close to you, or have in some way a life-altering experience. A severe trauma in any way can trigger a reason to embark on such a journey. It will feel like everything is collapsing. It is like we are shaken out of what we perceive as our reality, and the experience is changing our concept of life and the meaning that it has been given. There is an awakening happening. The one living the experience will most often not be aware of what he or she is going through. For me, it was profound. It was shredding me to pieces. I was being stripped of everything.

I became completely naked.

I was nothing.

I was NO thing!

In Matthew 7:13-14, Jesus spoke of travelling the narrow way. This might be seen as the dark night of the soul. It is a term that has been spoken of in many scriptures, and connects us to the endless experience of being close to Creation/God, and all that is. It is through the loss of self that one can find the inner truth and the feeling of eternal existence. The type of mental, emotional, or spiritual anguish that is present in the complete darkness, leaves the traveler feeling completely lost and alone.

This is the awakening to something deeper, a sense of real purpose, to true and real passion. It is like a death and a rebirth, where everything that *was* has now left, and new meanings, new concepts, and a new sense of existence arise. There is a death of the ego, yet nothing really dies except the ego's own sense of self. A very painful death, and the experience is that of death itself, even though nothing real died, and never will. It will feel like endless despair and darkness.

This is often a part of an awakening process, leaving us stronger and more true to ourselves than before. Once we have gone through the dark night of the soul, and have been "reborn", we can see that what was let go of was the false sense of self. What dies was never real, but we were clinging to it as a part of the illusion of ego. I remember the time as being completely heart breaking and mind scattering, yet it has been my most important learning experience as I see it.

Walking through the "dark night of the soul" is a time of spiritual purging and awakening, and a time of inner self contemplation and total aloneness.

The experience will typically show itself through these patterns:

- The ego dies, and the sense of self is shattered. It will feel like someone died, as they did, in a sense. The end of one's identification feels like losing oneself, and that feeling takes one to the deepest darkness. The old self has to die, for the true self to be born.

- The experience will teach complete aloneness. Through this complete aloneness one is shown that there is no such thing as being alone. We are all alone, yet we never are. True freedom emerges from losing the need to cling to others, or to feel one has to belong. The realization is that from feeling content in ones' own company, the love for others becomes stronger. Being alone becomes a beautiful thing, where much clarity is shown. The dependency on others disappears, and the value of meditation and solitude is realized. Being alone becomes a great part of growing and learning, and loneliness will get a whole new meaning. The realization that everything is within us, is true freedom.

- A new love for life is born. Everything seems brighter, and every life lived seems to be something to celebrate and to learn from. We are all mortal humans, yet we are immortal beings. The humbleness towards life itself becomes greater, and the love for living becomes even more precious.

- The way we see ourselves in the world changes. We become aware that we are all creators, and that we are not here to impress or to be what we think the world needs. We realize that the world needs people who are in love with themselves and life, and that will live in true passion and compassion. We realize that it is completely up to us, to take responsibility, and to live as the sovereign beings that we are. There are no one to blame, and there never was.

- The view of the world has changed, so one might feel there are different perceptions on the inside that are conflicting. Living in a world, when one sees the truth and it`s underlying agendas, can be a struggle. Through working on one`s own values, passions and authenticity, the inner balance will come.

- The strength from the experience will never leave you, and the new found inner confidence will affect every aspect of your life. This strength is like no other, as it comes from having "walked through the fire". You have been tested, and you passed the test. Now, all you have to do is to live the life you *know* that you deserve. You, we, everyone who has gone through the *dark night of the soul*, are stronger and more alive.

Like a Phoenix, we will rise from the ashes.

"Dear God, please help me. Show me the way to health, please show me the way. I am ready for complete healing. I am ready."

Here are some resources to explore on the topic of Dark Night of the Soul:
"Dark Night of the Soul", by St. John of the Cross and
"The Interior Castle", by St. Teresa of Avila

Chapter 6

Giving in and dying.

was experiencing what felt like death. Everything was dark, empty, there was nothing there. It was like my whole being died. My life seemed like this play that did not matter anymore, and who I thought I was, had nothing to do with my life. All of a sudden, all my beliefs were shredded. There was nothing to hold on to but *me* and creation. It was like nothing was important, and yet everything was. It was like I did not care if I was sick or healthy, and at the same time I had my inner most passionate drive to get well. Over a short period of time, I accepted that I had to leave everything behind. The feeling that arose within me, the inner *knowing* that I was part of something beyond this world, was powerful. It was like I was filled with this certainty that I could do this. That we could *all* do this.

From now on, this little quote would follow me:

"This too shall pass" – Osho

A whole new perspective opened within me. I had been listening to affirmations, but now I really saw the force that was behind them. I had to let go. I had to let go of everything! I had to let go of the need to take control of this. I needed to accept what my body was telling me, and trust it.

"If you're going through hell, keep going." - Winston Churchill

As long as our path is that of our true heart, it will always be the right one. The journey is ours alone, and only we ourselves, are the ones doing the walking. Life is never something that needs fixing, it is an experience and a blessing. Every experience holds value, and even when it might not seem that way, life is showing us something of great value. I was not here to judge or to keep track of the good and the bad. I was simply here to experience and to learn. I was shown this path to grow, and to let go. To grow *free*!

My life had been a mind trap. Like most, I was constantly thinking, analyzing, trying to figure things out. I believed that understanding was important. Understanding with the intellect. A wise friend of mine said not too long ago that every thought is an obstruction. How true that is. We tend to use our minds to set the standard of what we want to see in our life.

Feeling good is something we associate with certain outside events, externally created events. Although our conditioning has made us believe that this is how it is, we can break free from that belief. Feelings are not us, and we can choose, through the practice of letting go, to change them. Feeling good is a choice, and our life is created one thought, one belief, one feeling, and one bite of food at a time. The direction can be changed at any given moment. Wherever we are, at this moment, change will come. *We* are the key to creating our Universe, our reality. Never giving up, means to never stop valuing the amazing gift that life itself is. The endless potentials, the power that we all hold within, and the knowing that this too shall pass.

I was giving in, and that meant accepting that this was my life experience at this moment. I had to stop wanting out. I had to stop wanting everything to be different in the now. I was ready to accept and take full responsibility for my life. Pain, hurts, tears and all. Every single little bit of me, was ok. I did not care anymore. I was ready to let go of all that I was holding on to, and that was a lot! Loving myself had to be learned, and that was all that mattered. I was ready to love myself more every day, sick or healthy. The old programming needed to go. Most of us are carrying with us those old wounds from childhood. They shape our beliefs and our perception of our lives, leaving us with patterns that we keep living, over and over again. Mine were the typical good-girl-syndrome, and not loving myself. I was not shown that I was amazing or great. I was taught that I could do great things and look great. The value of *me,* was never shown to me. Not in a way that I could recognize. Not in a way that I could understand.

Lying in bed all day and night forced me to revisit every old wound that I had experienced in my life. The pain and the longings were all very real, even though they were outdated by my mind. A lifetime of suppressed feelings wanted to leave my emotional body, and I wondered more than once if I was going crazy. Was I losing my mind? In a sense I was, I was losing the old mind, losing the old programing. The road back would require some real emotional detoxification. The juicy stuff was yet to come. This was a warning that mind, body and spirit cannot be separated. They are one. My whole life, I was counting on them being separate, but no, nature was and is perfect, and so are we.

I really do believe that life begins after death, and that we are able to live to the fullest when we no longer fear it. I had been so ready to go, so ready to leave this life, that I felt free from the death trap. I no longer felt any fear of dying. It was not something that scared me or felt uncomfortable at all. I knew that I was more than this sick body, and that I would truly never die. I became more and more fearless, and it was setting my soul free.

The why's and the how's became less and less important to me. I just knew that I would have to keep walking. This was my life, and this was my responsibility. I was alive, and I was a mother. My children were not going to live without their mother, and that was that. If nothing else, that was what my mission in life would be, to be the best mother that I could, from here on out. Being a mother is serious business, and being a caregiver is the ultimate blessing. I was blessed, and I had to know it and feel it. I had to choose to live it, and to breathe it.

I moved on to swallowing Abraham/Hicks books like there was no tomorrow. These are books on how to change your life through changing your mindset and emotional vibration. On top of that, I was reading every other book I could get my hands on, on healing, mindset and consciousness. I started using binaural beats during my meditations, and brainwave entrainment CD's. These programs are designed to reprogram the subconscious mind. I also dived in to the whole Silva method program. I am not mentioning everything here, as it is not important at this time, but I was digging deeply into the mind-body connection. I was studying how to change our thought, change our mind, change our life. I was opening the door to the possibility that I, me, was the one that could change everything.

Every night I was talking to my cells. I was visualizing and planning. I was writing down my life manifest, and I was preparing for the future that I wanted to live. I had to un-believe most of my learnings and replace them with positive, empowering, lifesaving beliefs. My life was depending on it, and in the midst of my pain, I was up for the challenge. I was a part of this amazing creation and I was going to show myself worthy. I was not here to suffer, I was here to serve and to create. I had so much life left in me, and so many things yet to manifest.

Being alone was not the same as loneliness, I could see that now. I was alone, but no longer lonely.

I was still in bed, but I was on a mission. The tide had turned, the dark night was over, the light was back on, and I was up for it. It had been revealed to me that my life was my creation, and I was going to make it a good one.

Chapter 7

Alone.

"Dear God, please help me. Show me the way to health, please show me the way. I am ready for complete healing. I am ready."

My aloneness was no longer staring at me. Something was changing. Something had shifted in me, and it was as if I was no longer alone, even though I *was* in so many ways. I felt like I was connected with everything, and that I was always surrounded by spirit and superior support. In the physical, only a very few number of souls entered my room during this time. My husband, my children, a former friend, Stian, and my best friend May. That was it. I would have been lost without them.

When you are fatigued, meaning your adrenal glands are shut down, totally beaten up, hardly working at all, any little thing will cause stress in the body. It is like you are in a constant fight or flight mode, and all you need is peace and quiet. Understanding this, would have made all the difference for me. I would have seen that my symptoms were all connected, and that the solution was simple.

As simple as nature, yet as complex as a weakened and abused body can be.

When you are really, really sick, all you want is to be alone. I mean, not without friends or family, but any gathering of people will be exhausting. I noticed that the only people I was comfortable being around, were those that were not draining me, that were not there to gain from my energy. I had nothing left to give, and I needed to be filled up. I needed a refill on every level. This left me with a very short list of people. Not even a handful to be honest.

"Forgive them, for they know not what they do". Luke 23:34

The fact is that most of us hang on to what is familiar, and we tend to shy away from what is uncomfortable. My old friends were not comfortable being around a very sick person, and simply did not know how to respond to the different me. I was no longer the fix-it-all friend, and I was no longer the one you called upon for help and support. I was no longer the person that they were used to having in their lives. On top of that, I was too sick to have a conversation about trivial topics, and my interests were turning in a whole new direction. We tend to be afraid of the unknown, and the fear will keep us locked in the mind. Fear is never from the heart. It is always from the mind. I was no longer consuming any alcohol, and I was no longer the fun person to be around that they were used to. I believe I felt foreign to them, and the aloneness was something I had to experience. It was a part of my healing to let go of everything that was not serving me. Only true compassion and empathy can tear down the walls of fear of the unknown and unfamiliar.

I even had a therapist friend, who at one point told me she could no longer be my friend. She no longer believed in my healing, she said. She did not believe that I would make it, so she did not want to have any further contact with me. That was that, she told me. I was stumbled. As the message sank in, I could see her own fear shine through. It was off course a harsh experience for me at the time, but it was never about me. I know that now, and all she was doing was making me more determined, so I thank her for that. No one was going to tell me that I could not do this, and I knew that the message was about me being able to own my path 100%. I was being taught to walk my own walk, steady and firmly, and to not let anybody make me think I could not do it. Not ever. Everyone we meet is our teacher, but not always in the way that it first appears. Sometimes the true lesson will be shown after some time, and this was a great lesson for me. I had always been into what other people thought of me, and of what I was doing. It was a part of my programming.

I spent a lot of time working through the meaning of feeling left alone. It is a very common experience for those who have lived through prolonged sickness and isolation. At the time it felt like a cold shower. My friends and family stopped showing up, and I felt let down. All of a sudden no one was at our door. It had to be processed, it was my journey, and it had meaning. The whole scenario was a part of my awakening to *me*. It was a true blessing. I was able to set free what was not serving me, and invite in what was. Again, I was trying to hold on to the old, even though it was not good for me. I had to be shown very firmly. Like with everything else that I was experiencing, I had to be shown in capital letters, so to speak. I was learning to listen. I had been trying to hold on to old friends, even those who were not good for me, that were in fact draining me of energy, feeding off me.

I am in school, and I am learning a valuable lesson. I am learning the most valuable lesson so far, and I need to let them all go. Layer by layer, like peeling an onion, I am learning to set myself free.

It was never, and will never be about them, as it was always about me. Only me. I was the co-creator of my world, and I was the one drawing this very experience towards me.

I was focused at this time, and I was educating myself every single day. I was learning, and even though I tried to ignore it, I knew that I had to do something about my mouth. It had been hurting for a long time. I was ready to take on a very uncomfortable and scary task. I knew it had to be done. I had a wisdom tooth that was sitting firmly in my jaw. It did not seem to be heading towards my gum line at all. I was sensing there might be inflammation coming from the area as well, and I did not feel that I had a choice. It had to be surgically removed. I was not in any way, shape or form, ready for oral surgery, but I was firmly set on the task. "Get that tooth out, I am getting to the bottom of this!" I found a great surgeon that I trusted, my husband helped me to get there, and somehow I managed the whole ordeal without any complications or drama. Not that I was not ready to faint the whole way there, but I didn`t.

I am standing in front of the biggest change I could ever imagine. I am going from being a sufferer, to being a creator. I am laying down my sword to plant seeds instead, seeds of life. I am changing at the core, yet not changing at all. My true self wants to shine through, to come to the surface, and for that to happen, all of which is not serving me has to go. Who I really am wants to come forth. Finally, I am shredding what is not the true me. I am ready to let go of the masks. They are too heavy to wear. They are also too many to keep track of. It has been exhausting, and all I want is to be me. Authentically me. I cannot say that I am sure who that me is, but I am ready to find out.

The tooth was out, and I actually had another one removed that same year. Step by step I was clearing the space, giving my body less and less to worry about. My actions at this time might not all have been necessary, but it does not matter. They were all a great part of my education, and the intention was honest. I was being shown first hand, by the greatest teacher of all, the Creator. God was showing me the way, and I was determined to watch and listen. I was recognizing my body as my greatest friend and helper, and every single day I worked to show that I really loved it. I was going to spend all my time doing my very best.

I was going to spend every minute of every day walking towards what I knew could be done. I was going to get healthy, no matter what I had to do. I had nothing to lose. I was not afraid to die. My life had stopped as I knew it, and I now chose to find a new path. I had my husband, my children, my friend and I had *me*. I was blessed and I would do anything to be the best that I could be. Being a mother is an honor, and I was going to literally do anything to be the mother that my children deserved. I was going to get healthy, no matter what.

I was going to get healthy, or die trying.

PART THREE

THE ROAD BACK

Chapter 8

Getting set.

The road back for me, started the day that I *knew* that health would shine through. The day, or the time, that I could rest in that faith, was when the healing began. That was when the search was over, and the guidance became clearer. Still, in retrospect, the real road back had started long before that point. It started the day I decided to take charge of my own life, and dared to take the leap of faith. The day I took the very first step away from what was making me sick, is the day the road back started. There is no right or wrong, really, and there are no trials and errors. There are experiences only, and the labels we put on them. Trials and errors, if there were such things, are there for growth and learning. My walk towards health and healing has been adventurous, heartbreaking, educational, awakening, mind blowing and scary. It has been the ride of my life, and I hope that I will be able to share with you, the sense of the empowerment it holds, for all of us.

As I understood the importance of intent and focus, I made a vision board for my room. It is still on the same wall today. A lot of me went into making it. A vision board is a board, obviously, that you fill with pictures. The pictures are of what you want to create, so it can be a picture of a house that you want to manifest, or a place you would like to visit. It can be a picture that represents love and happiness in any way you perceive it. I was posting houses, people exercising, high heels and beaches. I even posted patio furniture that are identical to the ones I now have on my outdoor terrace. Yes, identical. The vision board was reminding me, every single day, of my mission. It was keeping me on point and on track. Such a powerful tool. Every time we focus on something, give our feelings and attention to it, we are ordering it from the menu of the Universe. Remember the old saying: "Be careful what you wish for, it might come true". I was counting on it, and I was ordering big time!

I was trying anything that sounded good and felt good. Herbs, supplements and therapies. My mission included a curious mind, and a willingness to believe in most, until proven useless. My first liquid fast was done from the day bed next to the vision board. I remember this so clearly. It was wintertime. Not that it matters, I mean the seasons came and went, but I remember there being short and dark days in Norway. I had read about juicing, and decided to do a juice fast. Not knowing anything about detoxification or kidney filtration, and not having any support on the subject, the ride was going to be a tough one.

This was the very first thing that I was led to do. You could say that I was going more or less directly from a typical standard diet to a juice fast. This was me, diving in, desperate and willing. I was not shy of any machine or device, so a juicer was already in place. My husband was doing the juicing every morning, leaving me with juices for the day on my nightstand. So, there I was, in my robe, my night stand filled with juices, and my determination being sharp and optimistic. I had to use my absolute will to drink only the juices for 21 whole days. I had to pull out my pure willpower. I was used to eating what everyone else was eating, and the hunger hit me badly on day 3. I ended up weak, skinny, and the fear of making myself sicker snuck up on me. There was absolutely no fat left on my body, and the experiment was over. I had no idea at that time, that my skinny look was from malabsorption, and that my body was showing me a weakness. I was proud though. 21 days on juices alone was not too shabby! I could do this, I knew it! I was not healed, not even remotely, but I knew I was on to something. This was when I first noticed that what I put in my mouth had an impact on my health, and that was profound! My body felt lighter not eating, much lighter. My stomach felt happy, and my fingers less swollen. This was actually a big revelation for my body. I did not know it at the time, but my cells had been able to rest and cleanse, if even for a very short time.

Food and me was on the agenda, and I dove into several ideas on the topic. I was, as you know, brought up on dairy and potatoes. A healthy diet to me would consist of all the typical whole foods, like fish, meat, dairy and eggs. To change my conception of nutrition and food, of what I was designed to want to eat, was the most important subject on this new agenda. School was in session, I had signed up, and the learning would happen by experiencing.

First stop, the elimination diet. An elimination diet is when you eliminate all foods that are looked upon as allergens, or that has a history of being trigger foods for inflammation. You end up eating a few different foods for a period of time, until you feel better. Then you re-introduce one food at the time, and are aware of the ones you are reacting too. I never felt better or worse on any one single food. Elimination diets did nothing for me. I was not even touching the surface of my problems. Had it only been this easy, I thought, not knowing that easy was exactly what it was, in reality. This theory builds on the removal of a food that is hurting you, because you are having an intolerant reaction to it. So you end up eating only fish and broccoli for example, even though none of them is going to help your body heal. As I would realize down the road, it was not so much about what I was putting in, but what I was not getting out. More truth was waiting for me. I had asked for complete healing, and that is a big question!

"Dear God, please help me. Show me the way to health, please show me the way. I am ready for complete healing. I am ready."

Being alone most of the time, helped me to focus. I was also connecting with other health seekers, a whole community of people seeking healing and remedy online. My husband was taking care of our son, and minding his career. Our relationship was turning into a practical one, and I was experiencing a deep sense of loss and neglect. I was recalling even more old hurts from childhood, and this period is colored by my aloneness and my longing for love. Even though I loved myself, I was longing for the community, the sense of belonging. I needed to be around people, pure and simple.

The internet became my world, and on *Cure Zone* I found Dr. Sutter. Cure Zone is an online forum where people group up to help each other and to share their experiences. Some, from having been sick themselves, and some from being practitioners that wanted to help. It was new to me that a person would help someone, a stranger, and want nothing in return. Dr. Sutter kept answering questions and encouraging hundreds of people, and he never seemed to tire. He inspired me. After being diagnosed with stage four liver cancer, and having been exposed to *agent orange* in Vietnam, he was now a healthy thriving chiropractor. Agent orange is an herbicide mixture used by the U.S. military during the Vietnam War. It contained a dangerous chemical contaminant called dioxin. Now, spending his life helping others get well, he was blessing many. I had found someone to turn to, and the support was unlimited. I believe that this was me learning that being in service is what life is really about. I was being conditioned to completely change the way that I saw the world, and the people in it. My heart was being opened, and my road back was not only mine after all. I would take many more with me, and we would walk together, in support and community.

He introduced me to parasites and liver flushes, so this was when I started to untangle my ill health. This was where I found my first mission, in cleaning my body from a heavy parasitic overload. It was something tangible. I had a specific task that I could focus on, one day at the time. I had tangled myself into this mess, I was going to untangle myself. Parasites he said, well, I read up on the subject. To me, at this point, nothing felt strange, to be honest. I had no filters and not a skeptical bone in my body, only a pure intent to do what I needed to do. My determination was strong; I could not be stopped. This is probably the most action filled part of my journey, right here. I mean, you will not believe what came out of me. *I* did not believe what came out of me!

"I had no idea that my body was a host for guests that I never knew I invited!"

Chapter 9

Uninvited guests.

After all those years of abuse, all those medications, and the intestinal imbalances, I was like a nest of parasites. We all have parasites, so don't freak out, and yes we *all* have them. I was going to find out just how much damage they can do when residing as uninvited guests. These little critters were baldly shown to me on the internet. Once you see a picture of some of them, you don't forget easily. I had no idea the havoc they could cause in any part of the body. They were having a ball inside of me, as I had a perfect house and I had been a fantastic host. They were thriving! They love an acidic environment. They feed on garbage, so to speak, on waste and toxins.

Like I said, we all have them, so if you are freaking out right now, don't. There are parasites in every living human body. They belong there, or some of them do. We are made of organisms, and every cell is alive. Every cell eats and poops. The same way any parasite does, the cells eat and eliminate waste. The waste that the parasites eliminate are very toxic though. They are hurting us by feeding off our nutrition and by excreting that toxic waste. They love to live in our mucus, our garbage.

There are a whole myriad of different parasites residing in a human body. 30% live in our digestive system, while the other 70% live spread out all over our bodies. This includes the blood and all organs, the brain and even our eyes and sinus cavities. I was totally mind-blown by this information. There are over 1,000 types of parasites that can live in the human body, and most often they are referred to as living in the intestines. Well known characters like ascarisworms, tapeworms and flukes are the most common ones. I had them all, in abundance. Some are large and easy to spot with the naked eye, though most parasites are microscopic. If you are hitting google right now, hold on to your hat and calm down. This is not for the faint, but for the troopers on a mission. A health mission will include any topic that needs to be addressed, and this topic was on my agenda for several years. Parasites alone will leave us feeling really sick, and *that* I can attest to. And as long as they are happy, they are not leaving.

My road back was definitely moving forward when I saw what was coming out of me during my heavy parasite cleanses. I had also discovered Dr. Hulda Clark. She was a Canadian physiologist and nutritionist, who spent her life researching and writing books on parasites and health. She had an herbal formula that I got hold of, and something started to happen. The parasites were not at all happy, they wanted to live, and I was feeling the symptoms. No one will give up their home without a fight, and my guests were no different. They were putting up a fight, a real battle. They are smart, and they are persistent. They lay eggs, and they have a life cycle that can last for months. Eggs can lie dormant, and I was told not to be fooled, but to remember this fact. So this is me, holding on to faith with one hand, while trying to hold on to my life with the other one.

The times were intense. I was seeing parasites come out of me, real parasites. Parasites and eggs, all different kinds. From what I had read I was the host of a large variety of different types, no longer welcome inside my body. I was wearing my robe, lying in bed, moving on to better and more potent herbal parasite formulas. Better out than in, is what I kept telling myself. Better out than in, and they were definitely coming out. All dead I must say, but still. You know that you are not mainstream, when you are looking for parasites in your stool. You also know that you will do anything to get to where you are going, when you are sitting in the bathroom every night with a tube of water going up your rectum. My enema bag was in heavy use, and the bathroom door was often locked. The enema bag was a must. I had to make sure that everything that needed to come out, was doing just that. A serious topic, but I am sure the whole setting would have made anyone smile, or run.

I am experiencing some dark times as the parasites cry for help. My emotional detoxing is confusing. I feel like I am losing my mind. My husband ensures me, I am not, and I am trusting that he is right.

Having been diagnosed with Lyme disease, I had added the Rife machine fairly early to my regimen. I was going for the big kill. A Rife machine is a frequency machine, invented by Royal Rife in the 1930`s. Simply put, his theory was that since everything has a frequency, one could find a frequency to kill any microbe in the human body. I had to explore and experiment. Remember, I was learning as I went along. I was at this point the killing warrior of the second floor. I was every living parasite's worst nightmare, and I was going to get even better at it. In practice, this machine is a little box-like device to put on a table. You are then connected to it by 4 cords going to both your hands and feet. I was putting my bare feet on some metal pads, and I was holding on to the hand-bars with my hands.

As my understanding and knowledge about the human body evolved, I found that the inner terrain was always alpha and omega. Simplicity was the key, and I found more and more truth on my path to Inspired. I sat in the hallway outside my room every day for two hours in the Rife machine. I was on a mission. I had the internet and my treatments, my books and my determination.

Together with killing off the parasites, I was getting ready to explore the liver and gallbladder flushing. It is not like I had this all lined up, but boy did it feel like it at times. Things seemed to be falling into place as I kept walking. It was as if I was following a written protocol. An invisible protocol. I was asking to be shown the way, and I was.

I had read that one should not do a liver flush with live parasites still inside the liver, and that made sense to me. The same woman, Dr. Hulda Clark, was also educating about flushing the liver and gallbladder. Many have walked in her footsteps, and many are still recognizing this as a great healing aid for a clogged up liver. Dr. Sutter had saved his liver by doing I believe close to 250 liver flushes, so I was confident, this was not going to hurt me. A clogged up liver does not sound good at all, and it is not. The liver is an organ of transmutation. By this, I mean that it changes one substance into another. Some of the toxins that enter the liver, are broken down and passed out of the body as waste. Others are actually changed into substances that the body can use.

The liver is not an elimination organ, but it is absolutely a detoxifying one. It is taking a big hit from the toxins that the body is trying to eliminate, and it gets clogged up from cholesterol and bile, forming small stones to protect us from the toxins. The word detoxification as well as its benefits, the physical and emotional crises involved with embarking on this journey, have been given a whole separate chapter in this book. It will simplify everything, and the understanding of the healing crises and detoxification symptoms are empowering and necessary.

Look at the liver as a large filter, with bile ducts that get clogged up with stones. I was definitely clogged up, from years of being medicated, from alcohol and less than optimal lifestyle choices. I was going to flush that liver clean!

I had also read that you should do this flush, which consists of Epsom salt, grapefruit juice and olive oil, until it produced no stones three times in a row. That, I must say, was going to take a long time. Two years to be specific. Yes, it took me two whole years until my liver said: "Ok, I am done." I was taking care of my uninvited guest, making sure that I got the eggs and the whole extended family, their visitors and all. For two years I was flushing my liver, killing the parasites, doing the enemas, and hanging on to the toilet. I will have to call this a quite intense period in my life.

Every 10-14 days, I did a liver flush, a total of 52 times, and then I stopped. I felt done. I had seen thousands of stones leave my body. Hard to believe, I know. It is the truth, and hard to forget. I do not believe that all those stones were initially inside my liver and gallbladder, but I believe that we keep making stones for as long as we are overly toxic. The body seems to be creating the stones to protect us. It uses bile to encapsulate parasites. I found them inside many stones. Yes, very true.

Did you know that the liver also represents anger, and that anger resides in the liver? To me, that was very interesting, and it gave me some deep revelations. I was most definitely invited to feel my anger during this period. I was not only angry, I was raging. I could get emotional releases that felt like volcanoes bursting out of me. Lifetimes of anger, all wanting to leave. The parasites were trying to hang on, dumping toxic gasses and waist as they were dying, making my whole body feel like a warzone. This was not for the faint, I knew that, but I had no other choice than to keep on going. I knew that it was my inner terrain that had to be changed, and I was working on it. When we have been abusive and ignorant to our health and body for such an immense period of time, the heavy methods are necessary. It felt like I was invaded, and I needed to clear the room - my body. I needed to restore the air, so that healing could accelerate.

I was cleaning up my diet as I went along. I did not jump from my typical much accepted supermarket diet, to a cleaner one overnight. It was not my main focus. It happened slowly, and over time. It crept up on me, and the cleaner diet found *me*, I did not find it. The diet coke had left, and I was naturally going vegan. That means I would shy away from anything that came from an animal. I was asking for simple soups, salads and juices, and that was it.

Looking back, I see this phase as my working phase. Every day I had a routine to follow. As you know, it took me two years to rid myself of all the parasites, and to get my liver clean. Had I known then what I know today, it would not have taken that long, but it was a part of my path and my experience. The parasites had to come out, and the work had to be done. I became used to living in my robe, sitting in the bathroom a lot, using the enema bag every day.

My joints were not showing any significant improvements yet, but I was moving forward. My inner voice was aligned with my actions for the first time since I could remember. I was actually doing what was best for me, and even though it did not always feel like I was moving forward, I had decided to trust that I was. Trust was my friend. Trust and faith are key ingredients on any kind of challenging mission. I had to find that inner knowing, the force of life that is within all of us.

"The body is a self-healing mechanism, and responds to everything that you do, say, eat, think, and feel." – Hilde

I was cleaning my house, my inner terrain. Cleaning out the garbage from head to toe. I was stirring up some heavy shit, literally speaking, and when that happens, hold on to your hat again! To have a clean, fresh, livable house, the garbage needs to come out. It does not matter how many nice things we bring into the home, or how much cleaning is done. If we never take out the trash, we will live in a stuffy, smelly, backed up, rotting place, crawling with uninvited guests. They will have a party, feeding off our inviting environment and hospitable lifestyle. I was detoxifying. Every minute of the day, my body was trying to get rid of some old garbage.

It was the toughest ride I had ever been on, and I had to hold on with all the strength that I had within! Again, separating the physical and the emotional is not possible. This became clearer and clearer to me, as my protocol and knowledge kept evolving. My path was showing me some slow and steady progress, but my mind was still looking for that day when I would wake up and say "Ok, I am feeling all better now". I was walking forward, but I had no idea for how long. I was taught not only patience, but also to handle and accept the uncertainty, the mental kind of uncertainty. School was in session.

NOTE: You will find the complete liver flush recipe and parasite cleansing information in my book "Know the Truth and get Healthy."

Chapter 10

Keep moving

was not exactly jumping around, taking long walks or riding a bike. I realized that my immobility was hurting me. I had next to zero movement during my day, and I needed to change that. Like Dr. Sutter had told me, even if I had to sit in a rocking chair, I had to get some movement. So I did, and in a rocking chair it was!

My room became a bit more action filled as I kept searching and learning. The portable infrared sauna was in place, and those sessions became a daily routine. I had studied these saunas, and they sounded great for detoxification. The far infrared rays will penetrate deep into the body, helping it to release toxins. Also, for me, not being able to move, I needed the sweat. My kidneys needed the help, and my skin needed the exercise. Every single day, I got myself into the sauna, with my head sticking up. Have you seen them? They look like a tent with a front zipper, and your head is sticking out at the top. I sat there for 30 minutes at the time, sweating, every single day.

Being bedridden has many challenges, and the lack of movement is one of them. The sweating, most likely, is what made me be able to survive the heavy detoxification I was putting my body through. The skin is the third kidney, and as my kidneys were down, slapped, and not very happy, the sweating saved the day. My sauna, since then, has been my good and trusted friend. From that first portable one, with my head sticking up, to a used one-person wooden stationary one, and finally a brand new state of the art shiny FIR sauna. I am still in love with my sauna, even though I only use it a couple of times a week now.

I can get dressed with some help, but my knees will only fit into these wide bohemian pants. I can no longer straighten my elbows or bend my knees. I need help getting in and out of a chair, and my feet need to be constantly elevated. I am dreaming of walking in shoes that fit me, of straight toes and slim knees. Being able to use a zipper, or put my hair up in a ponytail, all great wishes.

It was never really hard to keep my focus. My body was speaking so loudly to me it was impossible to ignore it. It was staring me in the face saying: "Here I am, and I need to be your number one priority." At this time, I am not sure if I can call myself motivated, or just being a machine. I did what I had to do, every day, as if I had found a destination point, and had programmed myself how to get there. I had the front seat, and was calling all the shots, but in reality I felt more like an observer. It was like I was just experiencing the ride, good bad and ugly. My challenge was to be able to not get mentally and intellectually unbalanced from all the symptoms that were accompanying the detoxification process of my body. When the road is long, and the valleys are many, losing sight of that road is a natural and human thing to do. Simply put, when it gets hard, it is human to want out. But when the going gets tough, the tough get going, and I *was*!

I had so much belief in the FIR energy, that I also added a Bio-Mat to my day bed. It's a high-tech negative ion and infrared ray treatment system that emits negative ions and far infrared rays. The gentle warmth of the Bio-Mat will give an overall massaging effect, and will aid in detoxification. It is a very heavy mat, filled with amethyst crystals. I always loved the crystals, and I am never too far from the healing energy that they emit.

I also got my hands on a chi machine, yes another machine! It is not the last one, but this one's a keeper. This little device became my great friend and personal helper. It lets your spine move from side to side, moving the lymph all through your body, while you are lying on the floor. I could do lying down, easily, it was my most popular position. Daily routine, lay down on the floor, and let the chi machine move your lymphatic system. I am solution oriented, so I placed it close to the stairwell that leads to the first floor. That way, I could manage it all by myself. I would sit down on the top step, and scoot myself along the floor. I could then scoot back on my rear end, and lift myself up with my feet two steps down the stairs. I could also measure my progress on how easy or hard it was for me to get up from the floor. It inspired me, as I kept my eye on the ball.

Moving meant more than being physical at this time, there was much work to be done to get the body back to its healthy natural state. Next task, the breast implants had to come out. Yes, I had those! They were beautiful, and I loved them, and they did not seem to cause any problems for my body. I had made my mind up though. This was not who I was anymore, and if there was even a fracture of doubt that my body was reacting to them, they had to come out. My surgeon thought I was crazy, but he did what I asked. Back home, there were no more breasts, many stitches, and I was feeling great about my choice. One more down, I was on a mission. This body was going to get what it needed, and nothing it did not.

I was getting more and more introduced to raw food as my diet choice. As I was studying health and healing, it made so much sense. I mean, hello, after all it was real natural food. Nothing more, nothing less. Food, just that, simple. I had been going down the medical route, the supplementation route, and I was now ready to simplify. I trusted the process, and followed every single hunch or intuitive hint.

This intuition of mine, or my inner guidance, led me to many different healers and teachers. One of them is a man that is working with homeopathic frequencies, and I had to explore. It was never my will that was holding me back, and sometimes I did not know my own limits. My home town is not exactly the center of the world, so travelling would be required if I wanted to explore. I decided I was going to see him, and so we did. My husband was always in. I cannot remember one single time where he said no, or we cannot do this. If I was in, he was in. He was so sure that I was going to make it, or at least that is what he kept telling me. If I wanted to go, we went. Me, in the car, with the seat all the way back to a downright position. Padded with blankets and pillows, feet up on the dashboard, in my woolen socks and bohemian pants. No shoes fit me at this point. Liters of juice to last me a few days were prepared and put in the trunk. I laid perfectly still, only disrupted by a visit to a gas station. I had to pee. I'm sure it's not often they've seen a woman being supported to the restroom, in the snow, wearing no shoes. I had to go, and that was that. Getting me from the car to the hotel room, and then to the appointment the next day, was quite a task, but we did it. We even ended up driving back several times, school was in session. I was constantly learning. What a ride!

My schedule was filled with my protocol, and my meditation time was the most precious time of the day. For 60 minutes every day, I'd lie down and reprogram my subconscious mind. Through subliminal programming, I was telling myself that I was worthy, that I was amazing and healthy. I was simply giving my subconscious mind less and less space for destructive thought-forms. I knew better now. I knew that everything I thought, would affect my life directly. The book "The Secret" was out, and that meant more fuel for my soul tank. I kept reading, watching movies, and listening to CD´s. I loved Eckhart Tolle`s book "A New earth". I read it as soon as it came out, and followed Oprah`s segment on it, on the Internet. I was on a spiritual path, and had no idea where it was leading. Not that I cared, it felt right.

For the first time, it was like I could sense home. It felt like walking towards something that I had been longing for my whole life. My path was chosen, and all I had to do was to keep on walking. I was being called, even though I could not grasp the whole message. Life was all about finding the strength and the determination that I needed to stay on course. I was saving my life, and even if I understood how sick I was and had been, I do not believe I was able to grasp the extreme changes that I would have to go through to come out on the other side.

"Through our actions, the momentum of movement, change and evolvement appears. We tend to analyze and talk about our visions more than actually walking our talk. If we truly want to serve, to give, and to empower ourselves and others, we need to act upon our visions. Being the change you want to see in the world, means acting accordingly to your ideal situation. Any change starts with a thought, a feeling, but only when connected to action will true manifestation happen." – Hilde

My next "Hilde is now moving no matter what"-step, was the full body vibration machine. I could stand on it, and it would do the rest. As the machine vibrates, it transmits energy to your body, forcing your muscles to contract and relax dozens of times each second. To me, that sounded like a great idea, and it was. The first time I went on, I thought my bottom was going to fall out. I had so much acidic waste stuck in my feet and legs that it hurt, big time. It was like shaking an open wound. I was on it though, every day, 3 times a day. I kept shaking it, and the pain left little by little. I was still on a mission, and I was telling myself that moving was my passion.

I remember jumping on trampolines from childhood. Back then, the only place to get a chance to jump, was in gym class at school. Now, they are available everywhere, in all different sizes. My eagerness was always way ahead of my physical ability, and this time was no different. I ordered a small trampoline, or rebounder, on the internet. It had a handrail. That way I could hold on while jumping. We got it all set up, adding yet another equipment to my regime. I was going to jump. I could smell freedom from just thinking about it. I must say, those little things are genius. I was able to start out by walking carefully onto the rebounder, holding on to the handrail, and then not actually jumping but softly doing an upward and downward motion. My feet never left the canvas. I counted every day. I counted how many times I could "jump" up and down. Progress is fun. I then moved on to how many minutes I could do, then actually letting my feet and myself, lift and flow. If you ever you think "I cannot do that", just walk towards it and take the first step. Then, think again!

Circulation of lymph does not come from physical movement alone. Although the body needs to move, it also has to have the circulation from energy and breath. We easily forget about our breath and most of us are shallow breathers. I know I was. That means that we breathe from our chest only, and do not fully draw the air all the way into our lungs, using our abdomen. The Indian culture is very aware of the healing power of the breath. Pranayama is an ancient practice of breathing control, and central in their healing regimen. I became a practicing student, connecting with my breath, while learning and exploring. Moving that lymph was helping me more than I knew, although I had yet to see the simplicity of it all.

I was doing what I had to do, and from not having anyone to guide me, except *me*, there was a lot of time spent trying everything that I could get my hands on. As you can see, I was piling up every machine and healing device out there, being my own guinea pig and experiment. I had no outer guidance, and I had no mapped out road ahead. My learning was my own, step by step, month by month. So, did I really need all those machines and tools? No, not at all, and yet they all helped me learn and grow. Like my oxygen chamber and my full body PEMF bench. Both amazing equipment for moving blood and lymph. The portable Hyperbaric Oxygen Chamber is a full body pressure tank that will increase the pressure of the air up to 1,5 times, and made me able to breathe 100% pure oxygen. The combination of increased pressure and oxygen content causes oxygen to dissolve into the bloodstream and body tissue, at up to 20 times the normal concentration. The saturation of oxygen in the blood that occurs during the therapy, allows the extra oxygen to be transported to the surrounding body tissues and organs. I found this while I was still not very mobile, and it sounded like an excellent addition to my healing regime. I was increasing the volume of oxygen dissolved in the blood plasma from the sessions in the tank. I learned the basic effects that it produces; It reduces the volume of gas bubbles in the blood, reduces edema and restores aerobic metabolism to ischemic tissue. It also aids in detoxification and strengthens our immune system and our ability to recognize invaders as bacteria and viruses. The PEMF bench, is a Pulsed Electromagnetic Field device that is also to increase blood flow and oxygenation. I had fun, and I treasure these devices.

My daily walks will always be what I will treasure the most from my road back. The day that I could start walking past the mailbox and the day I could put my feet in a pair of shoes and go outside, was the best day ever, so far. When it comes to movement, nothing beats walking. It is gentle, natural and healing. It was a huge milestone to be able to actually do what can be considered a walk. The forest behind our house has a trail. Several really, but there's a main one. It is not that long, but to me it was unreachable for years. What seems normal to most, can be the largest obstacle, and also the greatest wish, of another. This was what I was longing for the most, to be able to freely move around. Being so active all of my life, all the way from childhood, it was the greatest loss. A paradox? I can absolutely see the energy behind that.

What we fear the most, is often what we will manifest. The feeling of being trapped, of being imprisoned, was showing me what I had to let go of. What I had to work myself through, and transform in my life. Who knows how many lifetimes before this one, I had been experiencing some type of imprisonment. Now, I had a strong feeling of not being free, not being free to move.

True freedom is knowing that every moment holds great value, and that it never is about any goal or destination. It is all about each moment of movement, on the path called life.

I am moving along, still inflamed, spending each and every day doing my thing. I am eating the best I know how. I am sticking more and more to my raw food, my green smoothies and my juices. A lot of time is spent reading, studying and praying. I am meditating, keeping a journal, still holding on to the vision that one day, I will have an amazing life. I will feel amazing, and this will all be worth it. I will be able to run and ride my bike, to travel, swim, walk in the mountains and feel strong in every way. Wonderful loving people will enter my life. I know it, I am sensing it. I am driven by it, and I feel unstoppable. There is nothing that is going to take me back to where I came from. There is nothing that can take away what my heart is telling me. I know who I am, and I know I am on a mission.

I was passionate. I *am* passionate, and I believe I always was, about something. I was easily driven, and I still am. When I set out to do something, I do it. It almost killed me, and now it was saving my life. Two sides of the same coin. Life is like that. Yin and yang, dark and light, night and day, in and out, up and down. All a sign of duality. We need duality, it's what creates movement. It is what creates creation itself. I was seeing that what I had been told was a weakness, could also be a strength. I was embracing more of me, more of all of me, just the way I was.

When we are passionate about something, about anything, everything else fades.

Chapter 11

The spiritual connection.

"Thank you, body, for doing such an amazing job at healing yourself. I am so sorry for abusing you all those years. I did not know any better, but now I do. Please forgive me for not listening to you. Now I know better. I promise to respect you as my best friend going forward. I am sorry, please forgive me. We are a team!" Your friend, me.

Nature was calling me. It was really calling me. It started, not as a subtle whisper or a silent voice, oh no, it was a *big bang* kind of calling. One night, I was lying in bed, my night bed, getting ready to go to sleep, when it was like the whole Universe opened inside of me. When I closed my eyes, the most amazing thing happened. Mother earth flashed before my very eyes. I was seeing a glimpse of nature, and everything in it, inside of myself. Words cannot describe the vision and the colors. Trees, mountains, birds, flowers, waterfalls, the sounds, the smell, beyond this world, but not. It was like everything in nature was inside of *me*! Wow, I opened my eyes and it was gone. It was like I was being shown how grand creation is, and that *I* was a part of all that is. We, humans, are a part of everything that has ever been created! The vision has never left me to this date, and is clearly remembered as a part of my connection to spirit. I will tell you more about my visions, but first, a story about an experience that cannot be left untold. Nature really *was* calling me.

Through my reading and endless studies, I had read about Ayahuasca, the healing plant of the Amazon. Being bedridden and house bound, I was not seeing myself travelling to any South American country anytime soon. To be able to participate in a ceremony, a Shaman needs to be present, the plant was sacred, and only an experienced and educated being should perform a ceremony. What seemed like out of the blue, an e-mail found me. It was an invitation to an Ayahuasca ceremony in Holland, in Amsterdam. So close to me, but still a world apart. I remember thinking, well, we are going to have to do better than that. I cannot travel to Amsterdam, not at this time. I let it go, until another e-mail popped in. I really do not know how these e-mails found me. I did not remember connecting with anyone on the matter. I did not look at this as a very Norwegian thing to look into, but the e-mails found me anyway. This was a longing from my heart, a true calling from nature.

This new e-mail was from someone in Norway. There was going to be a ceremony deep in the woods, in a Lavvo, a wooden tent. A shaman with helpers were coming from Ecuador to lead the rituals, and they were bringing this sacred plant with them. Wow, I was really feeling called forth. My heart was pounding while I read all the information. I would still have to travel, by plane, train and car. How could I do that? Not by myself, that was for sure. I had to get my best friend and partner in crime to go with me. I sent her an e-mail, waited, and within 30 minutes she answered – "This looks cool, I am in, let`s go!" My heart was beating even harder now, wow, am I doing this? After being inside my house for so long, I was actually travelling AND seeing lots of people? "Can I do this?" My head was spinning. "Ok, I can do this, I am being called. I want to do this!"

I telephoned my husband. He knows me. His response to me after telling him I wanted travel to the deep woods, sleep on the floor of a Lavvo and get high on a plant from the Amazon was; "You can do it, go for it!". We were going!

What is Ayahuasca?

Ayahuasca (Banisteriopsis caap) is a vine of the jungle. It grows in the entire Amazonia, and is well known in Colombia, Peru, Bolivia, Ecuador, Brazil and Guyana. Shamans use this respected healing and teaching plant as the base of their traditional medicine.

I was so drawn to this whole idea, there was no going back for me. They say that the plant will be calling you forth, and it really was. Through dreams and visions, I was being pulled towards this plant and to nature itself. From my own research, I had found that Ayahuasca was boiled together with the leaves of a shrub called "Chacruna" (Psychotria viridis), and given during a ceremony of cleansing and purging. The mix in the brew, which can vary from shaman to shaman, is called Ayahuasca, and has been used for cleansing for more than 5000 years. It is also used to reach an amplified state of consciousness and a connection to source and inner demons. The Psychoactive effects of Ayahuasca is attributed to DTM (Dimenthyltryptamine). This is a substance that the body produces itself, and that is responsible for our vivid or nocturnal dreams. Chacruna is told to induce or connect with the visions, and the Ayahuasca plant is held accountable for the teachings and learning that comes from the experience.

Ayahuasca is consumed as a ritual in a ceremony, for healing purposes, and to solve any inner conflicts. It is used to heal the physical body, the mind and the soul. One is believed to communicate with spirit, and to reveal one's highest purpose under the influence of this plant. The purging involved, is the body letting go of any blockages holding one back on one's journey.

I read that research had shown that the consumption of Ayahuasca within a controlled context, showed no side effects, and that it was not addictive. The plant is used for spiritual purposes, and its characteristics would help us to reveal and let go of deep seated suppressed experiences and emotions. It is not by any means advised to consume this plant medicine without being in the care of an experienced Shaman.

The term Ayahyasca comes from the Quechua words "aya", meaning soul or spirit, and "huasca", meaning rope, or vine.

I was ready to take the leap of faith. Nature was reaching out its hand, and I was taking it. I was reminded of a channeling done for me many years earlier. This was when I was still on medications, searching left and right for some sort of meaning. The channeling was a very strong one, and it touched my heart. I was told that when I came back to this earth for this lifetime, I was asking Raphael to hold my hand. I was telling him, "Raphael, you better walk beside me during this lifetime, because it is going to be a bumpy ride. But I am up for it, I promise." This experience came back to me now, and I felt it was important that I remembered. It was like I was starting to remember my purpose. It felt like some locked away wisdoms and truths were going to be set free.

When your whole being is saying YES, you know you are on the right path. For me, who was still going through my emotional releases, peeling my onion, this feeling of enthusiasm was very welcome. Only a true calling and a quest for truth and healing, will lead two grown women to go on a plain, a train, in a car with a stranger, and sleep in a Lavvo in the middle of nowhere, throw up, and feel happy about it.

What do you tell your friends and family when you are going to a ceremony of this nature? While packing a backpack of warm clothes and a sleeping bag, the truth does seem a bit out of place. Well, we were going to a meditation retreat, a holistic gathering of some sort. It was to take place in the woods, so warm clothes were required, and the sleeping bag, well, we did not put too much focus on that. We felt like girl scouts on their way to camp. A tingling feeling of expectation, together with a feeling of uncertainness and uneasiness. Still, we were exited. This was a true leap of faith. The whole experience was going to be about just that, letting go and letting go. The trust had to be in God and nature, as we had no idea what was going to happen. Control was non-existent, and I was thinking; "Relax, nothing is under control."

One week prior to the ceremony, we were instructed to go on a specific diet. As we were both eating a vegan diet at the time, this did not change much for us personally, but there are some very strict diet recommendations for anyone wanting to participate in an Ayahuasca experience. This was reminding my inner being that I was on the right path.

Several types of medications will not go together with this plant. We were presented with a list of medical substances, as well as medical conditions that weren't a good match for attending this type of ceremony. Always consult your physician if on any type of medications.

We were advised to not drink alcohol or use any recreational drugs a week prior to the ceremony. Hot spices and red meat were also on the not-to-do list, together with very specific foods and herbs. Done, and done. We were ready, we were on our way, and the trip went smoothly. A helpful young man picked us up at the train station as planned, and he drove us far into the woods. We arrived a day later than our fellow medicine drinkers, thinking one night would be enough for us. That decision was never regretted by the way.

The place was beautiful. Right by a lake, in the midst of nature, this amazing large Lavvo was put up. It was a wooden one with a large open campfire in the center. We are talking heated floor, so yes, our kind of Lavvo. Mattresses were lined up all along the outer wall of the tent-like building, so it looked quite cozy. The other people there looked tired, and we would soon enough find out why.

We were appointed a spot each, and we put aside our gear. Mingling with the other participants, gathering information on what was ahead, I must say I did feel a little awkward at the time. I was not feeling my best, being nauseated, and my body was very uneasy. It was also hard to move, and I knew that I would have to need help getting on and off that mattress. There was no way I could get myself up from the floor without help. It was fine. May was there, and asking for help was ok.

The actual ceremony started at 8pm, and would go on for 12 hours, so no sleep was to be expected. Well, we went to camp, so there we go. "Faith Hilde, faith. You can do one night without sleep, you can do it." I was constantly talking to myself.

The well renowned Shaman from Ecuador was there together with his son and several helpers from Europe. As they prepared for the nightly event, they dressed up in colorful indigenous ceremonial clothing, and many participants started to play an instrument or to sing. We had all been invited to bring an instrument in the form of a drum or a flute, and we would soon be part of a wonderful sharing of heart-felt music and love. I watched, listened and enjoyed.

The fire was burning the whole time, and inside the Lavvo it was dark and smoky. As the evening approached, everyone, around 30 souls, found their mattresses and relaxed. Singing and playing was constantly a part of the preparation, and the Shaman was clearing the room, doing his ritual customs. My anticipation was rising, not knowing what we were going to experience during this long night. We were all given small buckets to keep in front of us. They were for purging, for throwing up. Not the most inviting thought, and not the most common setting I had ever experienced, but again, I was ready. This was where I had been led, and I trusted the process. School was on again, and trust and letting go was on the agenda. To even be in a setting like this was out of my comfort zone, and just by being there, I was pushing some boundaries, setting free some old patterns.

We were told that if we had to get up during the ceremony, to go to the bathroom (which was a privy, an outhouse), we were not to walk in front of anybody throwing up. Never to cross between that person and the fire in the middle. We were told that they could release spirits of a non-positive nature, that we did not want to take it in to our energy. It was also important to not go to sleep, and to sit upright as much as possible. If the experience got too intense, we were to look straight into the fire.

We were first given a potion with tobacco, to open up our sinuses and prepare for the Ayahuasca. It was given to us, on our palms, to be sniffed through our noses. Not a very pleasant experience, but that was ok. It felt like you can imagine it would. Pure tobacco water sniffed into your nose full force. Oh boy was it clearing those sinuses - burning hot!

So much was going on. The Shaman's helpers were constantly watching us, and the Shaman himself was doing his rituals. He was communicating with the spirit world, to bring healing and clarity to all the souls in the ceremony. The air was constantly warm, smoky and damp, smelling like burning wood and herbs. The darkness and the energies were intense. The ceremony had started, and the Ayahuascha was being brought to each of us. The shaman was blessing us as we were consuming the liquid medicine. He was standing in front of each one of us, talking, singing and using branches of wood to clear the energy.

I sat silently, waiting for the plant to enter my bloodstream. The psychoactive effects induce a modified state of consciousness, which is experienced in many different ways. Some get in contact with deep-rooted problems and others *see* their future, all that is, or energies from other realms. There are as many experiences as there are participants. Some find physical healing, and some can have a very traumatic experience. We had no idea what would happen to us at this point, so we just gave each other a silent smile, and looked at the fire.

From the point of no return, the nausea hit me with no mercy. I had never felt anything like it. The throwing up was constant, even though there was not much left to throw up. It is a different way of throwing up, a constant purging. You empty your stomach pretty fast, so we were told to drink small sips of water to have something to purge. The buckets were constantly exchanged for new, clean ones. The noise in the room was extreme, although the self-experience left one in a daze, and the rest of the room slowly faded. Time was lost, and the intensity of the moment was sharp and cruel.

Even though we were constantly aware of each other, May and I drifted into different states and stories. Still at the same time, our journey crossed several times, and we had many of the same experiences.

The first thing I notice after the throwing up subsides, is the flower of life. I have had this symbol around my neck for many years, and have been drawn to it for a long time. It is now floating around me, and around the whole Lavvo in a very strong greenish neon color. I am getting the feeling that it is the essence of all things, the core of existence. The core of existence! Being aware of the room I am in, I can see that all the other participants are shooting off energies towards the fire. It looks like they are all letting go of something, or releasing something, and it is going straight into the fire. It is a blue energy, shooting, like small arrows being released from the centers of their bodies. I am truly fascinated. I look over at May, half awake, half in an altered state of consciousness. She is still there. I am tired, tired and sick from purging. We are offered to drink another round of Ayahuasca. I consider it, and although I know this will not feel good, I ask for help to get up on my feet, and I drink it for a second time.

The purging is even more intense this time around, again, showing me no mercy. Then, in the midst of the experience, I feel calm and in total trust. There is no fear, no regrets, no thoughts, only the moment. I curl up on my side. I have to rest, just for a little bit. That is when I open up big time. It feels like my head is expanding to include all that is, and I find myself in the middle of the DNA structure. I am being shown the greatest change that is happening to mankind right now. I can clearly see our current DNA as black and white, encoded with the numbers 0, 1, and 2. It is shown to me as a string of 3- dimensional chains, where the numbers are floating in all shades of gray, from black to white. Then, I am shown the future DNA of man, the DNA that is now available, and of a true and pure heart-nature. The beauty is out of this world. It is made of all the colors there is, and many that I cannot even describe. All numbers are included, and I am told that this is what infinite possibility looks like. Infinite possibility, wow! I snap back to this awareness, and feel drained. It feels like some time has passed, but I have no idea how long I have been in that altered state of consciousness.

I have to go to the "bathroom". It is freezing cold outside, but it is truly a clear and blessed night. It is calm, and it feels like magic is in the air when I step out on the front terrace. The air is so crisp, and my cells are singing. They are in constant joy of the great news, of the knowing that true change has happened and that the potentials are present in this very moment.

I meet May outside, and although we share a few words, we are both in a state of just being and we wait until the next day to share our journeys.

It was a long night, but the no-sleeping-at-all part, went surprisingly well. The breakfast was served inside the Lavvo by some amazing helpers. It was a vegan meal with hot and cold dishes. Food was welcome, and a hot shower and a clean warm bed was on both of our wish lists. Eager to start our car, train, and plane trip home, we packed up after breakfast. We then caught a ride to the train station. Two tired souls, with a lot to share, who smelled like camp, had lived a very special experience. It would take some time for us to see the impact of the connection with the healing plant. They say that once ingested, the plant is part of you, and that, I believe.

In a subtle way, this is when my connection to nature really showed itself to me.

From having been all across the country, I was happy to be able to find my safe spot back on the second floor. I spent most of my time there still, but I was working myself down the stairs every day. Even though it was very hard to walk, I was now starting to go outside every single day. I found that I could wear Crocs, you know, those plastic shoes. They are not pretty, not warm, and certainly not made for fashion, but my feet could fit into them. That was all that mattered. They were giving me a new sense of freedom. They would be my shoes for a few years, the only kind I could wear except the open Birkenstock. So Crocs during winter, and Birkenstocks during summer it was. No matter the occasion, the outfit or the day of the week, those were my shoes. Do you remember that I said I was a shoe freak? True story. I adore shoes, I always have. Now, looks had to step aside, and comfort had to step up. I loved my Crocs.

I was making my daily walks sacred, and behind my house, in a small forest, I found my sanctuary. A new ritual was born, and even though the walks started out super short, and in pain, I was doing it! I was drawn to the woods, and it truly became my favorite part of the day.

My inner voice is changing from:
"Dear God, please help me. Show me the way to health, please show me the way. I am ready for complete healing. I am ready."

To:
"Show me the way, how can I serve, thank You for this healing."

I notice that when walking, the words are constantly playing in my head, like I am chanting.

There is a calmness that enters my being when I am outside. I have read about grounding, and I know the healing abilities of being grounded, but this was something more. This was me finding a new way to communicate with the divine. I was spoken to, and I was ready to listen. I think it started with the feathers. I call them *my* feathers. I cannot recall exactly when it first happened, but that's not important. I started to notice them on my daily walks. These were short 10 minute walks, only a few steps from my house, but I needed to get dressed, and I needed to get downstairs. The stairs were a struggle, but remember, I was on a mission. The rest of my days were filled with healing tasks, from diet to enemas. Determination was my strong side, and I was using it for everything it was worth.

Have you heard the quote "When angels are near, feathers appear"? I strongly believe it to be true.

The feathers started to appear on my every day walks. They would be planted in the ground in front of me, hanging on a branch I would have to cross, or simply sitting on my doorstep when I got back. Later, when I was walking in shopping malls and on busy town streets, they still kept appearing in front of me. I read up, and connected with the philosophy. Ever since, I have felt a strong connection with spirit, with the angels, when seeing a feather. I have a beautiful collection in my home, of some of the most special ones that have been given to me.

The feathers symbolize the wings of angels. They do not need wings to fly, so the wings represent their ability to carry out divine will. It is the belief that they will leave a feather when they are near. Many different cultures speak of the spiritual meaning of feathers. In addition to representing the actual feathers from angel wings, they are all referring to spiritual communication, and also the ascension to the higher realms. Doreen Virtue speaks about angels, and has done some amazing work with guided angel meditations. I am the owner of her books and CD`s, and I love how passionate she is about her sharing.

I had read that the ancient Egyptians believed feathers to be a symbol of Ma'at, the goddess of truth, justice, and order. The Native American chiefs wore feathers in their head-dresses to represent their communication with the spirit world. They also believed finding feathers were signs of new beginnings and rebirth from spirit. This to me, made me feel connected to those who had walked before me. The Celtic Druids wore ornately feathered robes to transcend the physical plane and gain celestial knowledge from the realms of spirit. In the Bible, feathers metaphorically represent loving care and protection. As a common dream-symbol, feathers signify the ability to freely move throughout life. Feathers can also represent a fresh start in a spiritual sense, as well as truth, speed, love, lightness, and flight.

This was uplifting and inspirational reading. It rang true with me, and I started to acknowledge the presence of spirit all around me. It was a bridging experience that lead to trust and faith. I knew that I was not alone, and I knew that I was being guided.

My dream world started to change bigtime. It was like going from dreaming to experiencing some profound messages and inner guidance. I will not make this a dream journal, but there are a few that I think will be of interest, and they are still clear and vivid inside of me. They were guiding me and showing me my passion. I believe that when we find our passion we find our place. Through passion we find our true calling. Mine is crystal clear to me now, but it had been hidden from me my whole life. I was slowly waking up to my real passion at this time. I was driven, and enthusiastic. My own health and healing had triggered an inner drive and a lust for life, that I never knew I had - at least not in the depths that I was now experiencing. This was breath taking, and I was feeling more and more humbled by what I was living.

I am in a grand forest. The trees are massive and tall. I am standing in front of a large round table. It is made of wood, and looks like it could have come from one single piece, from the cut of a huge tree-trunk. I am not alone, and I'm counting 13 of us. We are all standing around the table. There are no chairs. I tell the others that we all need to hold hands. The second we do so, our arms shoot up in the air, and a large flame projects, like a torch, shooting up from the middle of the table. At the same time the skies open, and the strongest most amazing sound I have ever heard is filling the air. I am sensing it is the sound of God, of heaven.

I opened my eyes, and I was still hearing that sound, like a frequency. Later, I have looked at it as being the HU. The HU is perceived as the love song for God.

"HU is woven into the language of life. It is the Sound of all sounds. It is the wind in the leaves, falling rain, thunder of jets, singing of birds, the awful rumble of a tornado. Its sound is heard in laughter, weeping, the din of city traffic, ocean waves, and the quiet rippling of a mountain stream. And yet, the word HU is not God. It is a word people anywhere can use to address the Originator of Life." – Eckankar

"I look at my feet as they walk through the woods. I am barefoot, and the ground is soft. I am walking on moss, surrounded by flowers and herbs. I am busy, and I have little time. Someone stops me, and wants to talk to me. "What are you doing?" They ask. I look down at my hands, and I find myself writing on stones. I am using a leaf as my pen, writing little sentences on each stone. "People are sick", I say, "and I need to write them what they must do. There are so many, and there is so little time."

This experience was short, yet very powerful. At the time I knew that I had to write it down. Much, much later, I see how great a message this is for me.

I continued to walk in nature every single day, and I still wore my Crocs. I now had a winter model, and was able to walk barefoot even during the coldest days. I stepped in and out of these shoes, no socks were needed. The feathers were still showing themselves to me, but not as often anymore. I was hugging the trees, speaking to them, and were they speaking back to me? Well, at least I was getting the message. Loud and clear. I was being told that I was on the right path, that nature is important to our healing.

We do not need to go into a forest to connect with spirit, or to do any type of ritual, but being outside truly does make it easier. The air, the sounds, the smells, are all connecting us to spirit.

My spiritual connection was always present. All through this walk that is my life, this journey, this experience of shifting my complete awareness of life, my spiritual connection was strong. I was led to events and people that would guide me to peel the onion, to lift the veil, so to speak. When we are shredding our shield, taking off our masks, the soul will become clearer. It will come through clearer. I was experiencing a sense of home in this connection. I was seeking to let every part of me heal, and in that process, the spiritual connection might have been the most important part of that journey.

I want to share an exciting experience I had, during a regression therapy session. The therapist was a very well known, controversial public figure here in Norway. I was curious as always, and booked a session when the opportunity arose. We met at his hotel room, and I laid down on the bed. Quite an unusual situation to be in, but I was drawn to explore. He was sitting beside me, talking to me in a low, calm voice. It was like I was drifting, but still being alert.

All of a sudden I see myself as this man, being carried by two other men. I am a captive, and I am hanging from two wooden poles, tied by my feet and hands. As they are walking, my lower back, the area around my tail bone, is constantly being bumped into the ground. I feel it fracturing. At that very moment, my feet and hands shoot to the air in real life, on the hotel-bed! I am totally experiencing this, in the now! I can smell everything, hear the sounds of people howling, laboring. I can feel the sun on my skin, and the pain. The very real pain! At the same time my body is reacting in this time and space.

I opened my eyes, and as I had seen myself hanging from these imaginary poles, the therapist told me I had been talking non-stop. I was lying on this bed, in this hotel room, with my feet and hands pointing at the ceiling. All four of them, straight up in the air. The experience was incredibly vivid. I rested my arms and feet, and said, "Wow, at least now I know why I was born with a deformed tailbone and lower back." You see, when I was born, my first vertebrates were not separated, they were always grown together. I have always known this; my whole life I have known that I was born with a *strange* lower spine.

Once I was getting a little better, being more mobile, I would have a lot of fun going to channeling workshops. My best friend would take me, making sure that I always had an extra chair for my feet, and that my food and water was close and available. I was drawn to channelings for a long time, and would later be channeling myself as well. Now, I mostly like to connect directly to source, and not through any other entities. If you are not familiar with channeling, it simply means that one connects with an entity, a non-human spirit, and communicate what they are bringing forth. It can be messages from your own higher self, or it can be from an arch angel or any other higher being. The workshops and experiences helped me to connect even more with myself, on all levels. Also, to feel that there is so much more to this life than what our naked eye can perceive, was always freeing to me. It always gave me a sense of freedom.

My husband will never forget some of the incidents that took place in our home. During the time of cleaning out all and everything from my life, strange things would happen for sure. We had spirits that literally moved our heaviest appliances, like the washer and dryer. Moved them, as in several feet, in one go. Indeed, not for the faint, but luckily I have had several really good helpers. Clearing the house, our space, had to be done many times, and every time something was let go of.

While on the topic of strange experiences, I will share one that stayed with me for a while. I have later had out-of-body experiences, and this might have been an opening in that direction;

I wake up as I am being laid down on my bed. From above, lowered onto my bed, I feel the bump when my body lands on the mattress. Someone or something grabs my feet, holds them down. At the same time, I am pulled towards the end of the bed, at a very high speed, although I am not physically moving. I open my eyes in shock. Someone is still holding my feet. I look over to see if my husband is lying next to me. If he is, this is not a dream, I am awake. He is. I am breathing, not making a sound, paralyzed. Breathing until it lets go of me.

We are not our bodies we are eternal beings. We are spiritual beings having a human experience. Not the other way around. I knew that I was not my body. I knew that I, as in *me*, as in what I could feel was my true essence, would never die. Also, I knew that while I was in this body, on this Earth, at this time, I could live in a healthy body, we all could. I knew that health is natural, and that we are all able to heal and regenerate.

We ARE a part of God/Creation, and the closer to home we get, the easier it is to feel the whisper of truth.

Chapter 12

Unstoppable.

I cannot lift my arms to put my hair up, and I cannot hold a pen to properly write my name. I am witnessing that I have no choice but to go "all in". I have no time to lose, yet time is all I have. I have no alternative, as there is no going back to where I came from. The future is in everything I do in this moment.

It might seem like there was no progress, it sure felt like there wasn`t, but there was, always. If it was not visible to the eye, it was noticeable emotionally or mentally. I was seeing little things - like not needing to sleep 16 hours a day, or to be able to sleep through the night. We tend to not notice the subtle changes until we look back. My digestion was better, no more constipation, and my anxiety was slowly fading. I had been on the empowering Ayahuasca trip, and boy did that make an impact on my self-esteem. I had seen the true power of who we were, and I had mastered the trip itself! How amazing was that? I had been out there, in the real world, well, not the most real thing for most maybe, but quite an endeavor.

I was filled with a sense of purpose now. As I kept on walking towards health every day, I spent more and more time helping others. I am not a professional, or in any way a practitioner, but I am sharing the experiences that I have gathered so far. It gives meaning. To be able to contribute means the world to me. From being totally dependent on others, or at least that's what it felt like, I can now contribute in a small way. My time on the Internet moves from solely being about me and my healing, to being about how I can help and cheer on someone else. There are always those who are worse off than ourselves, and I was finding that the suffering out there was endless. Sadly, I was not alone in my struggles. So many people were seeking remedy, and so many were searching for health. I was living in a very sick world, and being able to help, inspired me to keep going.

My studying became more structured. I was filled with a determination to gather knowledge and truth, and as long as I was slowly getting better, I felt I was on to something important. Still focusing on my healing, never straying from my daily healing routine, I was led to put my studying to work, so to speak. My business was gone, and I had left everything that I believed would be my future. Now, I was seeing a small glimpse of a new one, a different path. I had a vision. I had hope, of someday being able to help others like myself. I had been longing for support, and I wanted to become that for others. This was my new focus. I would study and heal, and I would be able to help and inspire. No one should go through something like this alone.

I had to keep working on my patience. As there is no magic bullet to real health, the body will take its time to throw out everything that is obstructing the energy. That means that it has to take out *all* the garbage, the toxins, the parasites, heavy metals and acidic waste. Mine was trying to release *everything*, but my organs of elimination were not functioning as they should. They were tired and beaten down by drugs and rock' n roll. This manifested itself in extra pain, tiredness, inflammation and more. The detoxification symptoms can be tough, and as I was learning slowly but steadily, I also had to hold myself back. I was used to going full speed, and I was not learning anything the easy way. This realization has been invaluable when coaching clients and writing my step by step book *"Know the Truth and get Healthy."* Detoxification is not a topic to be taken lightly, as detoxification is an art. It will lead to a healing path, but it can throw you off like you will not believe. Now I know.

Between the enemas and saunas, my walks, the time on my Bio-Mat, my eating and my meditations, I still studied. I read everything I could find that resonated with me on healing, health, raw food, parasites, nutrition and spiritual growth. I read about ancient practices, and made my own tinctures and raw crackers. I was experimenting. I always loved a good experiment. Being fearless to me, means not being afraid to try anything new, once. It also means to be curious and to not take anything too seriously. This quality was an immense help, when using trial and error on how my body would react to different supplements and treatments. I believe in talking about what I have experienced, and not only what I have read in a book or article. Books are great, truly, but the most powerful learning is always in the experience. Every experience holds great value no matter what it is. I was trying to honor all of mine.

I knew that I was unstoppable, in the sense that nothing could get me to back down. A true healing journey is a path of determination and perseverance. It is important to flow and to let go, but without the plan of action or the ongoing will to move forward, there will be no driving force. I had to not only let go, visualize and rest, I also had to *do* what was necessary to support my body. I had to constantly work on my emotions and my old patterns. I had to physically move and eat what was in sync with a healthy organism. My mind, my emotions and my physical being, all had to be supported and embraced by *me*.

We are our own best friend, and at times our own worst enemy. We know this so well, and so did I. I knew that there were patterns in me that were holding me locked in a situation of ill health. I knew that I had manifested this *lack of freedom*. True health is a term that I look at as true freedom, and breaking free is a choice. I had made mine. The very day that I decided I was done doing and living what was keeping me sick and lost, I had made that choice. I had empowered myself bigtime, without even knowing it. At that moment I was indeed unstoppable. I was unable to stop, although that does not mean that the experience of ups and downs, frustration and dark times would not happen. It most certainly would.

The *"there is no magic pill"*, will have to be learned and lived, yet it will never stop those who have made the choice.

As I was seeing more and more truth, and was awakening more and more to what nature was showing me, I could see that only *I* could ever stop me, and I would not, ever.

Chapter 13

Raw for life.

The raw foods were speaking to me like old friends. I do not remember exactly how that happened, but my diet was changing step by step. All by itself, it was changing. It had gone from the typically cooked, pizza, hot-dog, diet coke diet, to a cooked vegan style cuisine. I had been juicing and experimenting with fasting, but the raw living natural foods kept knocking on my door. I was reading everything I could find on the matter, and ordered all of David Wolfe`s books and programs. I was drawn to it. My whole perception of food and nutrition was changing fast now, and my spirit and body was loving it. Again, as the mind, body and spirit cannot be separated, what was right for a healing body, had to come forth. I had asked for healing, and through every little step and revelation, I was finding a piece of the puzzle. A puzzle I was starting to see the beauty of. Still, I had no idea how many pieces I would need, or how to find them all. It felt like I had been starting from scratch, or from less than scratch actually. It felt like I had started from below zero, recreating my whole life and body. From feeling the lowest imaginable, the victory of seeing the light is beyond description. By carefully watching every sign and offering of information put in front of me, I was led to these amazing truths about our bodies and lives. Truth will set you free, even if it at first it most often will piss you off.

Raw food makes my heart sing. It is like every cell is thanking me, saying, yes, yes, yes! It is like the topic is an awakening in itself. So simple, so obvious, and so natural. If you have ever been passionate about anything, you will know what I am talking about.

First of all, what *is* raw food? I know, a silly question maybe, but a very common one. We have wandered so far from our natural way of living, that it does not seem natural for most of the human population. Did you know that the human body is designed to eat raw fruits and vegetables, that this truly is our natural diet? We are a tropical species, we are primates. Much more on this later, if you keep walking with me towards Inspired and free.

Raw food, is simply put, food that has not been cooked, or in any other way altered from its natural raw state. That means it cannot be heated past 47 degrees Celsius, or 115 degrees Fahrenheit. At these temperatures the fruits and vegetables will keep their enzymes and nutritional value intact. On top of that, they are keeping their energy, the God given, life giving energy. We know that everything has a vibration, a frequency, and every cell of our body is affected by the frequency we put in to it. Raw food is simply food. It is simply food as nature intended, being everything we need, period. That is all. No list of ingredients, and nothing added that we do not need. All pure, perfectly put together food, vibration, nutrition and love. Like every other species on this planet, we have been blessed with foods that will nourish and heal. Foods that will cleanse and hydrate, strengthen and regenerate. How amazing is that?

The most amazing thing about raw foods is not what it is, but what it is not.

Raw food is pure and natural food, and it contains the simple sugars that feed our cells, not our parasites. The body will not create mucus in the need to get rid of it, or because we have irritated the mucosa, and the parasites will have no playgrounds to play on. To see and experience the terror that the body is going through from being exposed to dairy, gluten, meats and processed food, is soul wrenching. The simple yet so hard to grasp fact, that the body is made in the same manner as any other mammal or primate, to thrive on raw living foods, is a deal breaker for many. The social conditioning is so strong, that breaking free from the eating complex is most often harder than not, despite the will of healing. The parasites and the underlying emotional hurts are too strong to conquer. Well, I tell you my friends, do not despair. Truth is truth, and there is nothing that an empowered mind and being cannot do. One step at the time, as I did - anyone can.

I was lead to raw foods, as I was seeking truth. I was seeking true health and vitality. I was asking; "Show me the way", and I was shown. I was shown the simple way, the easy way, and the natural way. I was finding my way back home, through re-connecting with nature and creation.

The first thing I noticed when I stopped all the cooked foods was that my digestion got better. Not over night, but I remember when I noticed it had *really* gotten better; It was on one of our first very short trips after I had lied down and stayed there. We had borrowed a beautiful little cabin by the sea, and I managed to sit in the car for the 3 hours it took to get there. There was no way I was getting out if the car during the ferry ride, so I hid in my seat. At one point we stopped at a gas station. I was well on my way to a clean eating diet, but I was not 100% diligent. I accepted mashed potatoes as a fast on-the-go meal, and - wow! That whole night, I was in terrible pain, and I had forgotten what that felt like. Everything was coming back to me. The nightmare of ulcers and digestive pain, so vivid and clear. I was *not* going back there! So, that was that, raw it was. My stomach was happy, and that is always the first step towards healing. I knew this, and I was shocked at how my body was rejecting cooked starch and dairy. Yes, the mashed potatoes had dairy in it. Just smashing.

As my digestion kept getting better, my energy was getting better, and my outlook on life was changing. From this point, I was going all in with the raw. I was staying on clean organic fruits, berries, vegetables, nuts and seeds. I was hooked. I was not going back.

The truth shall set you free!

I was setting myself free from old beliefs and programming about what the body needs to thrive, and as school was in session, I was open to receive. My knowledge was pointing in the same direction as my experience, and that is truly a powerful combination. My compassion for animals was evolving as I got cleaner and more educated. I've always said "when we know better, we can do better". I was going to do better. Every single day of my life, I was going to do better.

"I am sorry, please forgive me, I love you, thank you! – Ho`oponopono.

I was seeing all this suffering, and all this pain. I had come to realize that very few can see the connection between the food we eat, the lives we live, and the suffering we embark and experience. It became obvious to me that the animals eat to live, while humans most often live to eat. Eating can be a spiritual experience, and what we eat can kill us. It is often a reflection on how we feel on the inside, a reflection on our emotions. Also, food is not just food. It can be love, fulfillment and spiritual contentment or enlightenment. On my path I still meet people who would rather eat what makes them sick, than to get well. The programming is too deep, it's hard to break free. So many diets are thrown at us through magazines and books. Even our governments are offering nutritional advice, and we follow. All the way to *Sick-Ville* we follow. They offer slimness and happiness.

Slim is happy, right? They offer us the life we believe we want, and the body we think is going to give us eternal inner peace. Also they offer the solution to our failing willpower. Easy to do, and an easy fix is what this world is all about. The food industry contributes to over-eating, then try to sell us a slimming diet or product.

Nobody tells us to love ourselves, and that loving oneself is the key to a better health and a stronger body.

All this focus on different diets shows us how lost we are. How disconnected we are from ourselves. Primary foods are something everybody need to feel fulfilled. Primary foods are the food we eat, the love we receive and give, the confidence we feel, the spiritual nourishment we get, and the creative input and freedom we give ourselves to create.

The foods we eat are secondary to everything else that feed us; our relationships, career, spirituality, and exercise routine. At the same time, they are the key we have been searching for, as you will no longer harm what you now love. Raw living foods will raise the vibration and the awareness, and also magnify the feeling of love and compassion.

Once I started to nourish myself, to feed my cells what they needed, and stopped eating what was hurting me, my body celebrated. It was finally able to start the healing process, the hydration and the regeneration of cells and tissue.

We are disconnected from our own inner knowledge about what the right foods for us to eat are. We are a part of nature, and we know what we need the same way an animal does, a wild animal that is. We have just forgotten. Instead of acting like the sovereign beings that we are, we look to an authority for answers. That is the way our society has been evolving, or disconnecting rather. We are so used to looking outside ourselves for answers, that we will jump at any authority`s statement on foods and health. That is an act of victimhood, and victims we are not.

We are in charge of everything we do, say, and certainly what we eat. I was aware that I had a choice, I was not aware that I was not making a conscious one. I was waking up to the responsibility and the logic behind life and health, but I could also see the wall of misinformation and social conditioning that was present. I had chosen the road less travelled, and maybe even the road not travelled. I had not yet met someone who had walked before me, whom had healed from where I had started, so I knew that my guidance had to come from the inside. No one could tell me; "*I had rheumatoid arthritis and now I am healed,*" or "*I was nearly dead from Lyme, and now I am living a healthy beautiful life.*" The answer would come from within, as well as the guidance and the support. All from trusting and having faith.

The information that is out there is a creation of the mind, of the intellect. The wisdom lies within the heart, in the DNA, and we can access it through being still and trusting ourselves. That being said, there are so many toxins in what is presented as food today, that our system has gone into addiction mode. This addiction is the number one killer in the world today.

The sugars that are present in our so called foods is very addictive. It gives us a false craving for more, and to connect with what our body really needs becomes impossible. Most often when we are hungry, it is not real hunger. We are feeding our parasites and our addictions. The complex sugars are feeding fungus and parasites both. The adrenalin in meat, and the salt and the coffee are boosting the adrenals, while at the same time destroying them, declining our health and vitality. A supermarket is filled with sparkling labels and addictive foods to keep us coming back, and to keep us from waking up to the true masters that we are. A master is not a follower, and a follower is what makes the profit. With ingredients that our grandparents would not be able to pronounce, and nothing that nature intended us to eat, the body will shut down its most precious life-force. Sickness is taking a hold, and medications are next. A grim truth that I know only too well.

Change starts with awareness, and by what we are putting in our mouths. When we eat to live, we go from surviving to thriving!

This is something to ponder: When someone has a challenge with food, it is a combined physical and emotional problem. Weak glands, candida and parasites will send the body signals to keep feeding the cause. It is also a lack of self-love issue; the *I am never good enough*-illusion. A stressful job and a dysfunctional relationship can also easily determine how we eat.

What is going on with us, since we are not taking care of our bodies? What emotional need are we trying to satisfy?

It is never about the food when we are on binges. It is always about *us*. So, one way to resolve an unhealthy eating habit, is to change things in our lives that are not working the way we would like them to. Once we start cleaning out your bodies, our mind and emotions *will* follow. Our true inner knowing will shine through, and we will *know* what is right for us. We always know, we always did, we just need to remember. We are *frugivores*, and we are designed to eat living foods. Think about it, we are all part of the same creation, the same Mother Earth. We must trust our ability to choose what is best for us, and power up on that!

We can eat for health, for sickness, for spirituality, for the environment and for the animals. It is always your choice. IT ALL IS! I knew this, and I was making a better one.

"When we love ourselves just the way we are, we start to treat ourselves like a loved one, the best way we know how." Hilde

Chapter 14

All in.

Back to my story. As I kept walking, my passion for the raw living foods just kept on growing. The more I fed my body with these organic fruits and vegetables, the more it craved them. I was studying the pH miracle, and was determined to give it my all. To be able to really feel what this could do, I had to go all in. I decided to stop everything else that I was putting into my body in form of supplements, to really clean my physical body the alkaline way. I had been using zeolite, chlorella, different herbs, amino acids, vitamins, minerals and much more. If it was out there and sounded like a good idea, I had tried it. Some of it valuable and good, most of it not. Today, I live by a very short list, seeing that less is more and that isolates never win. The body does not recognize an isolate, so again, nature is perfect.

When I go all in, that means all in, always. I was going for the all liquid 3 months, all greens, all raw, all blended kind of commitment. I learned that as the blood needs to stay alkaline, with a pH (power of Hydrogen) at around 7.4. By feeding the body alkalizing foods, the blood will stay alkaline without having to take these alkaline minerals from our tissue. The theory is that the alkaline food is going to alkalize the whole body, so that it can heal itself. I know, very simplified and not really science, but on this diet/protocol the focus was the pH. This pH focused diet was raw, but it was going to exclude all fruits and berries. The theory being that sugars are acidic. On top of that, it was promoting a high intake of oils and salt, so my calories would come from avocados and oils. The salt was in theory what my cells needed for energy, and little did I know that this theory would almost kill me.

The body is the true healer. Only the body can do any balancing and regeneration. To even be discussing diet shows us how far we have wandered from our true selves and the truth of nature. What species would have to wonder and discuss, and even get agitated over what food is best for them? This is what the mind can do. We are over-thinkers. Our mind is a tricky thing, it will lie and deceive. The truth is in the pudding we say, and I believe it is. In the experience, and in the open heart, truth will find us.

Back to my alkaline diet. I was following it to the tee, but I saw no real change. I had already been at this for a few years, the raw, so this new protocol was fairly easy for me to follow. The difference from what I was already eating, were all the fats and the high salt intake. Even though a bell was ringing, and drinking oils by the bottle did not feel right, I kept following what I had set out to do. I tend to do that. My digestion was suffering bigtime. I was also on several supplements as a part of this protocol. Drinking massive amounts of water. I am talking a minimum of 6 liters a day, filled with a green powder. I was popping Vitamin D3, B12, and ingesting large amounts of sodium bicarbonate. Yes, it is alkaline, but the stomach is not. I was hurting.

Not giving up on anything I had started, we did what I thought would be impossible at the time. My husband dusted off our suitcases, and off we went from Norway to California! Yes, on three airplanes, sitting for God knows how many hours, airports and wheelchairs. Raw food in the hand luggage, and prayers in our hearts. It was the most challenging thing for me, maybe ever. I had no idea how I was going to make it across the globe. Me, who was now used to being close to my bed, my house and my machines, was going to California? The crazy Lavvo trip was one thing, but now my heart was pounding even faster. We ordered a wheelchair for all the airports, and I was wheeled from gate to gate. A new experience, which taught me more than I had bargained for. People did not look me in the eye, and even the customs officials asked my husband questions regarding me, as if I was not even there. "Hey, I have a hard time walking, but I am fully awake!" I was left facing a wall, not being able to see what was going on, and I felt so much compassion for my fellow wheelers. I was left grateful for the much needed assistance, and most of the people I met that were working as helpers, were nothing but beautiful.

This was going to change everything, or so I thought. I was sold on the idea that we needed to stay away from the sugary fruits, and that they were somehow bad for us. My husband and I stayed in California for a month, with me eating liquid green foods only. On top of that there were daily colonics and massages. I was drinking oils by the bottle and was injected with sodium bicarbonate intravenously. I was doing this program big time, and yet, I got home feeling that something was off. This was not natural.

Nature knew better than this, and I knew better than this! Only man would believe that fruits were not good for a human body, and only a human would believe that isolated chemistry, in the form of bicarbonate would be something that the body would need. I was ready to break free from the theories and trust that truth would reveal itself to me. The fear that I felt just thinking about eating fresh berries and fruits, showed me that I too had been a self-submitted *victim* of the brain game. I was fearful that the fruits and berries were going to harm me, but at the same time, I knew that this was all in my head. Nature makes no mistakes, and I needed to cut myself loose from these protocols. Simplicity Hilde, listen, simplicity.

I gave thanks for the experience, for the teachings and extra knowledge, but I knew that I had to simplify and trust in mother nature even more. I had to up my level of trust. I was trusting, but not totally. I was still running after symptoms and pills, and I was still being fed fear-based information. I was still listening to the marketing forces of the health industry.

When someone tries to tell you to do as they preach, or you will forever stay sick - run. When someone tells you that nature made a mistake, and that man-made products will fix you - run even faster. Truth is always shared from a compassionate state of love, as it is speaking to your heart. Fear cannot speak to the heart, it speaks from and to the mind.

"Show me the way, how can I serve, thank you for this healing."

I can see that now, that my path, my road back, and my story, had to include it all. It really had to be the long and experience-filled road that it has been. Without it, I would have missed all the colorful nuances, and all the self-experienced knowledge. I would not have known how it felt to be depressed, to have anxiety, to expel parasites and liver stones. I would not have known about wanting to die, or how feeling alone really felt. Severe pain would have been foreign to me, and I would not have been able to know what suffering felt like. I would not have felt how the different diets, raw or not, were affecting the body, and I would not have tried and experienced most machines and healing modalities out there.

"My ability to recognize my own experience in that of another, is what will be of true value".

Back from my trip to California, I was ready to take the next step on my mission. I was ready to break free from the mind game once and for all. I was diving in to everything out there on Raw foods and healing. I was educating myself even more on veganism, seeing more and more truths about diet and so called disease. The more I read and experienced, the more I felt free. "Is this the freedom I have been seeking?" I was sensing it was. I was sensing an inner joy and a new form of inspiration. This was no longer about me and my health, I *was* getting my health back, it was already happening. This was about so much more. This was my mission and my passion melting together. It was like remembering why I am here, what my life purpose is.

The trip had been of great value. My mind was clear, and the whispering that I had been hearing was getting even clearer. I knew what I had to do, and this might sound funny, I knew I had to eat fruits, and yes, it scared the shit out of me. There was so much resistance, so much reluctance, it was not even funny. I had been told by several of the so called health gurus out there that fruits were not good for us. Not only were they not good for *me*, I would never ever get well if I ate them. Fruits had too much sugars, and were acidic. Fruits would kill me, literally. Fear was imprinted in me from what I saw as an authority. Me, following someone else`s fear based information still? Yes, I was, and I was not eager to admit it. No more, no more.

I had awakened to the energy of food for life. The simple solution to all our dietary needs is so obvious, yet at the same time, the hardest thing for most of us to embrace.

I was seeking solutions, not intellectual reasoning.
I was seeking truth, not old beliefs.
I was seeking freedom, not criticism.
I was seeking health, not cultural traditions.
I was seeking empowerment, not mass conditioning.

The answer was simplicity through raw, living, high vibrating, healing, natural, organic, food. Whole, organic and fresh. The longer I stayed raw, the better I felt.

"Truth is simple, change is hard." Hilde

Chapter 15

Stepping up.

A new chapter was upon me. I was signing up with IIN, Institute for Integrative Nutrition. I was going to be a Certified Health Coach. I had decided to channel my energy towards a certification, still helping others, and letting the divine keep opening the doors for me. I would be able to study from my home, though a virtual classroom. I would meet like-minded friends, and learn from top teachers from around the world. What a blessing! *And* I was letting my own body heal, *and* I was educating myself. I would be able to learn and help others at the same time. I knew that it would be hard at times to keep my focus, and to do the exams while my body was detoxing and cleaning itself out, but I was excited! There was a clear purpose behind this endeavor, and I would be able to channel my learning into something tangible. So much suffering was out there, and I wanted to help. The wind of change was blowing, and I was eager to contribute in any way that I could.

From not knowing where to go, what to do, or how to do it, I now had one thing down; I knew what to do, at least for now. It felt like a huge part of my mission, and it was. I had seen myself being able to do this, and the day that I took the leap of faith was a joyous one. Being clear on what you want is very important on any journey. I knew what I wanted, there was never a doubt in my mind. I wanted life, I wanted to live. I wanted to live pain free, and I wanted to be able to help others. I wanted to feel what real health felt like, as I had never had that feeling, not really. It was crystal clear. My body was a self-healing mechanism, and my life was my co-creation. I was the captain of this ship, and I was the one responsible for the voyage. I had been seeking for the compass and the map, but was sensing I already had it inside me. It had been there all along.

I was eager to start the classes, but at the same time I was sensing some tension. The little girl in me was showing herself, afraid she would have to be perfect again. Always having to be at the top of her class, always having such high expectations. I could assure her right away, that this time it was different. We were at a different place now, and the learning came from a place of passion and enthusiasm. We were doing this out of love and interest, not for recognition or a high score. That being said, I never did or will ever stop trying to do my very best. That is within my nature, and I love it. I simply love to expand and to see how much I can do. I dive into new tasks with the eagerness to do my very best, always. This time was not different. I studied hard, and I had fun doing it.

This school and study was just what I needed. I was able to tap into 101 different dietary philosophies, learn about how to empower others. I was now part of a larger community of likeminded people from all over the world. My perspective kept expanding, and my knowledge was growing. Being a raw food explorer already, having lived what I had lived, made the journey even more interesting. I already had experiences that I could use in my discernment. Also most of the presenters and speakers were already known to me. It made the process flow smoothly - even through my rough detox periods. Oh yes, the detox periods. I will tell you more about them in a later chapter, but going from HELL to Inspired is a bumpy ride. Bumpy as in ups and downs both physically, mentally and emotionally. I was not let off the hook easily.

I knew enough about detoxification to know that I was one toxic puppy. I was experiencing every symptom you can imagine at this time. From killing off yeast and parasites, to eliminating acids and heavy metals, I was downright feeling terrible a lot of the time. I was getting stronger, so I knew I was on the right path, but the rollercoaster ride was quite scary at times. I was to experience every little bit of it, so stay tuned for the inside on detoxification, and how it is necessary to save your life.

At this time my knees are still stuck being swollen to the point where I cannot wear regular pants. They had not shown any sign of movement the last 3 years, and the inflammation, or what used to be fluids, seemed to have turned into a hardened mass, like jelly. My doctor had tried earlier to do a synovial fluid tap, but the liquid was what he described as too thick. No needle could get it out. I was now thinking it could take years and years for my body to dissolve this, so I needed to have it removed. My knees were deteriorating fast now, and something had to give.

I gave in, I caved. I agreed to have surgery on both knees to clean them out, and they were scheduled only three months apart. I know, how could I, right? Well, I needed this to be over with. It was a hard decision to make, as my mind and lifestyle was set on the body doing all the healing. I was going back to the hospital with all the bad memories, and I had said I never would go back. This was a tough one. I was struggling. My mind was telling me it was the right thing to do, yet my soul was crying. What an inner struggle. I went for it, head on, I trusted that it would all turn out fine.

This time I have brought with me my raw food, and I know who I am. I am on a mission, remember? This will not be a popularity ride, as being different most often is not the most popular thing. I know this, and it is ok. I do not want to eat their food, and that is taken as an insult. The fellow health seekers and roommates are fairly curios about my food and lifestyle. The staff in white, not so much. I am given cold shoulders from simply saying "No thank you". I am politely declining their food offerings. "I have brought my own, I am fine thank you.". That was it, I always try to be as anonymous as I can about my diet. It was not possible, it is spoken of, loudly. Do I believe I know better than them, or that what they are serving is not good enough? That is the energy that meets me. I say nothing. I drink my juices and I eat my own foods. I speak very little, and I keep my focus. I am here to help my knees, not to move in and make friends. I know, a cold attitude, but I am protecting myself. I have been here before. This time I am stronger.

The experience is soul wrenching. Full anesthesia, and I would come back for more. One knee down, waiting three months, then back for the second surgery. No compassion in sight, and I am back to those hallways of sickness and hopelessness. Everything I had experienced is coming back to me. This time I am armed. The detoxification symptoms that arises in a cleansing body is not for the faint. When we are clean, the body will set in full force to clean anything that resembles toxicity, or is in any way harmful to the organism. Wow, I had no idea the body would react to the toxins in such a quick and extreme manner. I am sick as a dog. The pain comes back, and my body is ready to purge. The day after the surgery, both of them, I say "No more meds". I know that getting off all chemicals is important for me. I cannot feed this cleansing body any medications what so ever. The surgery was bad enough, so it had to stop. I will let my body go back to rest now. I have to forgive myself.

"When you stop what is hurting it, the body will start to cleanse, heal and restore." Hilde

I am most definitely purging toxins. Once the medicine/chemical is not going in, the release starts. It is almost instant! I politely decline the evening doses of pain medication, and the next morning, BAM! I am so sick! I am throwing up, having diarrhea and a low grade fever. Me not accepting any more drugs is not popular though. What about my pain, do I think pain is fun? I tell them I am fine, that I do not have that much pain, really. They do not believe me, and having the track record of being the disobedient patient does not help the situation. I am being investigated. What am I doing, and why am I not on any medications? I feel a storm coming. I am uneasy. I am not on my own territory. I feel out of place.

Two doctors show up at my bedside to ask the same questions. "Why are you not on your RA medication, and why are you refusing the painkilling Valium?" *Indeed, why am I not? Well, so many reasons, but I just smile and say:* "I am working on getting healthy, and I'm doing something different. It is working out better for me, and the pain right now is manageable, I am fine."

I understand that my answer is not accepted as a final one, and the head of this hospital, the chief doctor has been alerted. I hear rumors of this, and I know what is up when I see her entering our room. My 4 roommates are here, and they line up to get the latest on the freaky want-to-be-healthy patient. There is no privacy to be had, or so I find out. Let us all discuss private matters in an open forum, shall we? Standing at the end of my bed, in front of all of us, this woman in white gives me a 15minute long speech on how I am killing myself; "Your joints will slowly deform, and all of your organs will deteriorate. You are hurting yourself, and I hope you know how stupid and reckless you are. Who do you think you are? Is your family aware that you are not taking your medications?" *She is going on about how irresponsible I am, and how she has to warn me, that getting better with no medications will never ever happen.*

Her hands are uneasy and constantly flickering in her pockets. Her face is red when she continues: "I am an educated Doctor, and I hope you know what you are doing by going against my protocol. Know that you are slowly killing yourself!" *The fact that what she had offered me nearly killed me, is of no concern it seems. The fact that she offered nothing but drugs and surgery, never comes up. The fact that all of her drugged-down patients are having surgeries to correct their deformed and deteriorated joints seems to have slipped her mind. She speaks her mind and leaves. This has been a monolog, not a discussion.*

I say nothing, I just let her finish her speech. I am on a mission, and I know within the deepest of my soul that I am on my way to health and vitality. That is not what she or her protocol is offering. It is 100% clear to me, that her approach is not that of true healing or compassion. Love is not present here, not in expression. I thank her for showing that to me. I thank her for making me even more determined.

I am being reminded again that every single person that we meet is our teacher. She is showing me my strength, and my inner calm. I am my own authority, and I have taken responsibility for my life. After the speech from the head of operations, I am no longer of any interest to them. The next day, I silently, and very anonymously, leave this hospital.

I leave for the very last time, more confident than ever. I have been shown the alternative, what I walked away from. I am never going back. Life is too short. I am going for the vitality and the expression of truthful living. This is not honest nor true. This is a reflection of power and greed, money and an enormous industry. This is my perception, this is my experience.

I am very grateful for the surgeries, even though they did not produce what I had been hoping for. The swelling never went down, and after about 6 months, they were back to the same size as before. I had gone through two surgeries which produced nothing, or nothing that I could see as valuable at the time. I would just have to trust that my body would get to my knees before they deteriorated more. The ultrasound taken at the hospital had shown that there was degeneration going on, bigtime, in both knees. I was told by my surgeon that he expected me back within a year, for a full knee replacement of both knees.

We were not on the same page, and a knee replacement was *not* what I was seeing. The displayed joints were not for me. I was on a mission!

I was long into my raw food path, and I was sensing a whisper of change. I was true to my greens, meaning a high fat, non-fruit raw diet. Yes, I was still on my no fruit diet, even though I knew it might not be optimal for me. I had been feeling uneasy about the diet since we came back from California, and I had been asking the Spirit for guidance. I was being poked and put to the test bigtime. I was led to read about water fasting, and I felt eager to dig deeper, to step it up even further. A water fast is serious business, and will induce some deep cleansing. I believed I was ready. I was ready to embark on a water fast.

Actually, all the way back when I was lost and with no direction other than running from what *was*, I did a 6-day water fast. My cigarettes and I drank only water for 6 days. No food, only water. I would not recommend including the cigarettes, but my soul was on to something. Animals in the wild will lay down and stop eating when they are in the need of healing. They will let the body use all its vitality and energy on that one task. We use as much as 70-80% of our energy to digest food, so no wonder we are tired and want to rest after eating a heavy cooked meal. This is also why fresh fruits and vegetables are amazing for the human body. They are what the body is designed to easily digest. They nurture, digest easily, hydrate and bring in the true life-force.

I was preparing for my fast by making sure I would not be disturbed. I planned to spend the fasting period in bed, resting as much as I could. I was gathering some good books to read, and some movies to watch. I knew I could do this, and I was eager to see what it could do for my health. This was the summer of 2012, and it was, without me knowing, another turning point in my journey. The fast is rough. I was climbing the ladder too quickly. Too many toxins were being released for my body to handle. A water fast is the top of the mountain, it`s a very potent tool, and will allow the body dig really deep. The cleaner you eat, the lighter, the higher the vibration, the more healing will take place.

That means that if you are eating a typical western processed food diet, a more healing diet would be a whole foods diet. Even better, a dairy free, gluten free diet. The next step would be to move to a vegan diet, then a raw food diet, then a low fat raw food diet, and a mono eating diet (eating only one food at the time). Last would be juices only, and then water fasting. Top of the mountain!

My water fasting was giving me a lot of symptoms. Besides being extremely fatigued, I had no bowel movement at all during my fast. For 16 days I drank water, read, meditated and slept. I felt like crap, and I was getting terrible rashes towards the end. My kidneys were clearly showing me they were not yet up for this task. My elimination organs were not able to secrete what I was stirring up. I was skin and bone, and I was not comfortable continuing. This is the downside of being thin from the get go. I never had much fat on me. I had always appreciated a lean body, and by being athletic, working out on a regular basis all my life, I stayed slim. I was, for the first time in my life, wishing that I had some fat on me. I was led to end the fast on day 16, so that is what I did. Not a very eventful trial, but a new experience to learn from. I was not yet 100% ready for a water fast.

I do not recommend anyone embark on a water fast for more than 3 days without proper supervision. I am not a doctor, and I'm not intending this to be medical advice.

"When the seeds are watered and nurtured, growth is inevitable". Hilde

I had been poked with Dr. Robert Morse`s videos on You tube. As I was listening to his videos I knew it was truth being spoken, but my mind and my soul was at war. I was literally getting nauseated from even thinking about eating fruits. For three years straight I had been following this so called alkaline, no fruit, high fat diet, and I was now being led to let it go completely. At the same time, I had to recognize that what I had been doing might not have been the best for me. I had been on a raw food diet for about 3,5 years, but it had been filled with oils, salt and supplements. I had been lingering in a mind game, and a symptom chasing regime.

I was ready for the leap now, and I couldn't be stopped. I had been asking to be shown the way, and I was. I was also asking for guidance, an inner guidance. I was answered loud and clear. Trust in nature, it is never mistaken. I was reading "the Essene Gospel of peace". It was mailed to me by a stranger. Thank you, thank you, thank you.

Excerpt from The Essene New Testament; Jesus said: *"God giveth the grains and the fruits of the earth for food; and for righteous man truly there is no other lawful sustenance for the body.... For God is just and bountiful who ordaineth that man shall live by the fruits and seeds of the earth alone."*

I had been to Florida several times during the last few years. The first trip was during the spring of 2011. I was able to travel business class, and was wheeled everywhere. We even had a wheelchair to take me from the car to the hotel room. The hotel was providing the wheels. The stay was pretty much about sitting by the pool and being pushed around in shopping malls. The rest of the time was spent in the room. I was happy though, I was seeing and experiencing new things. The next trip was during that same year. We repeated the previous route pretty much, loving the heat and the Floridian energy. The heat was at the same time a burden to my sick body. I had no energy to handle it, but since I had lived in Florida during those early years, it was like my second home. It was forever precious to me. It always made me feel like I belonged. Norway is not exactly raw food restaurant heaven, nor shopping for fresh organic produce paradise. Florida was in comparison - true magic!

At the same time, I was taking my exams at IIN, and reading and studying every moment I got. I graduated that spring, and was now a certified health and Wellness Coach.

Next time, in September of 2012, I was going to see Dr. Morse, and I was eager. As I love to study, I had read his book prior to the visit and I was well informed on his passion. Something about him was calling me, and I was listening. I was ready to simplify and to let go even more, it was time, it was *my* time to hit the shift button!

I knew that this man would be able to be of great support to me. *Boy* was I in for a surprise! This man was no support, he was so much more! The compassionate being that he is, and the honest willingness to help, blew my mind. I was humbled and honored to meet him, and when I left him that first time, I was no longer holding on to any old fear. I was calm and focused, and I knew that I had gotten a new friend, a real one. I found mutual respect and connection to the whole staff at the clinic in Port Charlotte, Florida, and I honor them, and thank them all for being a true light in this world. (Shannon, you know I love you!)

I had found yet another teacher, and this time, it was like coming home full circle. Everything that I'd been walking towards, and everything that I had been studying had led me to this point. My search for simplicity and genuine healing lead me to the simple understanding of how the body works. It led me to the inner knowing that all I had to do was to remember, and most importantly: get out of my own way. I needed to get out of my mind, and into my heart. Fully and completely. Nature *is* perfect, and I kept growing free.

I walk through a discrete glass door in a low Plaza building along what seems to be a sleeping area of little Port Charlotte, Florida. A young man greets me from behind a small reception area. The walls are covered with photographs of Dr. Morse and his mentors. The atmosphere is calm and inviting. It has been a long travel, but I am here. I am feeling eager and anxious at the same time. I am still having a hard time standing on my feet for too long, so I sit down, hold on to my banana, and drink my water. When Dr. Morse enters the room, he does so with a great smile, open arms, and I am soon embraced in a long and warm hug. I know this soul, and I am happy to finally meet him again. His energy lights up the room, and his smile is from his heart. The next two hours are spent analyzing my eyes, talking about my health history, and mapping out my herbal protocol. My diet is already optimal for healing, and my daily routine has all that I need, and nothing I do not. I notice while listening to him, that he never tires of the health and healing topic. Like me, his burning passion is keeping him focused, and his heart is genuine and open. I know that I am blessed. I know that my prayers have been answered. I've been shown the way, all the way to a small building in a very small town across the world.

Herbs are added to my life, and together with the wild greens and herbs that I have already been picking, this was fueling the start of a passionate path for me. The wild edible path. I will get back to the amazing wild edible herbs, and their healing and regenerative properties. The wild edibles are the most potent greens for vitality and nutrition, and now I was adding these dried and tinctured formulas, made with love and 40 years of experience. They were put together to support my weak organs and glands. Herbs are tissue-specific and have a high conscious awareness.

The topic had invited me in since my Ayahuasca experience, and I could clearly see that my dreams and visions were connected to this path. I was listening, and I was receiving loud and clear.

The herbs were pushing my body into a deeper state of detoxification. I was experiencing heavier symptoms of cleansing now. My lips were swelling, and my eyes were red and inflamed. My head was congested, and the acids were on the move. Remember, I was a heavy diet coke drinker, filled with Aspartame, the neurotoxin from hell. I had been using the steroid eye-drops for years, paired with Botox. On top of that I had added the toxic hair coloring, the skin lotions, the heavy duty cleaning products and so on. The more I lived, the more I had to I re-live. My memory was feeding me more and more lifestyle choices that had contributed to my total crash. I gave my body a new role in the new book of life that I was writing. It was the star that would endure and conquer anything. My body was my hero.

I was eating my fruits all day long now, feeling the raise of energy, and the absence of pain. I was completely and utterly in love with the juicy, colorful, tasty, hydrating fruits. All fear of nature`s wonders had left me, and my cells were singing the Hallelujah while doing the happy dance. I was starting to remember what pain-free felt like. I *had* been pain free, I just had to go way back to find that time. Remembering the past is fine, but I was not going that way, so I was looking straight ahead. I was spending my energy on eating my fruits, and blending in some leafy tender greens now and then.

The simplicity that I was blessed by seeing, was like a key to the inner most hidden box of truth. Never had I heard someone speak directly to my inner knowing before. My whole being knew that I was home, so to speak, that truth was there, and that I could trust the process 100%. The search was over, and the pondering, the learning and the educating was not going to be the same anymore. My head was done for now, and my heart had taken over.

My more evolved senses were eager to step up, as I was ready to step aside.

Dr. Morse, my friend and mentor for many years now, is still a guiding light for many, blessing us with his wisdom and experience. Through his International School of detoxification, I am now a certified Detoxification specialist, Level 1 and 2, and I keep showing up for Dr. Morse's classes. My cells never tire of hearing truth, and my heart will never tire of the spiritual connection that is present.

This new lifestyle, if one can call it that, was fueling my enthusiasm while it could easily be a challenge for others. I was convinced that when people around me saw that I was healing, and that I was walking towards having a life again, they would be eager to know what I was doing. To me it would seem natural to want to cheer this change on, and to get involved in my journey. Instead, I observed that most people are afraid of the new and unknown. They do not at all appreciate that someone is stepping out of the norm. To see someone eating a diet completely different from their own, can be very challenging. I learned that by making different choices, I was excluding myself from the community, so to speak. From simply not doing what had made me sick, I was threatening the common belief system. I was healing myself. I was going from HELL to Inspired. I was out of bed, looking and feeling better. I was still the freak, and my healing was the elephant in the room. No one wanted to talk about it. The topic felt uneasy. To this very day this is my experience, and it shows us how deeply conditioned we are to hold on to what is.

I had gotten used to bringing my own food to parties and gatherings, and that was fine. Getting together is always superior of any diet or food choice. When my mother wanted to make a special dinner for me and my husband to celebrate our 25th anniversary, I was pleased and appreciative. When she told me she wanted to serve meatballs, after I had been raw for five years, it really dawned on me; What I was doing was my journey alone. No one else's, but mine. It was my responsibility, and mine alone. I politely declined the invitation, and I was grateful that I am able to choose for *me*. I've got this!

One of the most popular topics that I came across when people noticed that I was eating a different diet than them, was the protein question. "Where do you get your protein?" If there was ever something we have been imprinted with needing, it is protein. Never mind it is most likely what we need the least, we are told to make sure we get a lot of protein. Most people have no idea how their body works, obviously, and they are not at all educated in nutrition. No special skills in healing or meal planning, but protein is something most people know about. We need our protein. It is a fact. We need lots of protein to build muscle and to stay strong. It does not matter that it comes from a burger with fries, it is still good for us. Yeah, right.

Skipping the long story; No, we do *not* need any protein from any animal source, in fact, the body is hurting every time it is presented such heavily dense "food". The old programming is outdated, and an upgrade is needed. We actually do not need much protein at all, and answering the popular protein question is easy;

The short version, for those not really interested, is:" Where do you believe that the animals you are eating got their protein?".

That will most often end the conversation. When one is genuinely interested, the answer would be something like:" Your body does not use protein, it builds its own. Just like a horse, an elephant, a cow or a gorilla, it makes protein from amino acids. All the amino acids are found in the plant kingdom, in fruits, berries, vegetables, nuts and seeds. When the body is served a complete animal protein, it has to first break it down, to look for the amino acids, taxing the kidneys, our most precious organ for eliminating lymphatic waste. Look at it this way; Ingesting the protein is like feeding the body a brick wall, when what it needs is the brick. Now, it has to tear down the wall, clean the bricks, and get rid of the mortar - representing the metabolic waste created from breaking down animal protein."

I am still running into the question quite often, but awareness is shining through. More compassion and more understanding of what we as humans are designed to eat is growing. We are slowly getting more aware, and I am confident that change is blowing on all levels.

When we know better, we can do better.

Everything we will ever need as far as nutrients, comes from a plant source. Why would we believe that we needed to go through the killing and eating of an animal, to get to those nutrients? The meat industry has a large number of the population believing that meat is a nutritional source, and that even milk from a cow, made for calves, would have benefits for a human baby. The industry then has us hooked on it, and drinking milk from an animal, is normalized all the way into old age. A very sick, calcified, painful and debilitating old age, for the vast majority of people in the Western World today.

Nature is perfect.

We tend to get fearful that we are lacking nutrients, when the plant world offers the most amazing variety of them. Like every other species, you as a human being, will never lack anything if you're eating raw living foods. This is what we were meant to eat, it is not a man-made diet. Reminding me of yet another myth; We supposedly evolved into eating cooked foods, and cooked foods are better for us. What? How would killing the enzymes, depleting it of most of the nutrients and altering the chemistry ever benefit anything? How could chemically altering nature be of benefit to a living body of more than 100 trillion live cells?

Nature IS perfect!

When we realize this, there really is no need for any animal to suffer. There is no need to keep eating acidifying, mucus forming and disease forming foods. Nothing good will come from it. This is our time to rise above, to shine, to get healthy, free and in sync with Mother nature - once again.

Cause and effect is a law of nature, and that also means that what you eat affects your body. It is all energy, and everything holds a vibration. That is nature at its best. It is a natural part of this amazing creation that we are all a part of. I hear the "I need more protein", or "I do not do well on vegetables", or "I this and I that". Why would we be different? Why would we not eat and thrive on the same exact thing?

Think about it. Here we are as humans, being born with identical chemistry, in the sense that we all have the same composition of organs. Our glands and bodily functions are all the same. On the inside we do not differ at all. Every baby that is born will drink mothers milk if available, and if not, it will still be given the same to drink. After that, still the same as every other child in the same culture. If we look at nature, all species eat the same within their kind or their species. Every lion has the same diet, and every gorilla does too. I am sure they do not even know their blood type. Do you know that while humans have four general groups of blood types, horses have ten? A, C, D, K, P, Q, T, U, V, and W polymorphisms. They all eat the same foods, no matter their blood type or any other factor.

153

We are only as different as our weaknesses. That means that we are created equal, but have been passed down weaknesses from our parents. Animals do not typically have our lifestyle generated weaknesses, and therefore they all thrive on the same species-specific diet.

We cannot improve nature, only raise our vibration to get in sync with it.

We can easily define the difference between Carnivores, Omnivores, Herbivores, and Frugivores. They all have different teeth, intestines and stomach, saliva production, stomach acids, general physique, and much more. These differences are indicating what they eat, and how they are able to gather and hunt their food. It also indicates how they are able to break down the food to utilize and eliminate it.

Carnivores kill other animals with their claws and tear them apart, eating primarily their organs and drinking their blood. A lion is a Carnivore. Omnivores will eat from the plant *and* the animal kingdom. A bear is an omnivore. Herbivores eat only green plants and herbs. Some of them are also grazers, like the cows. A giraffe is an herbivore.

Frugivores eat primarily fruits, berries, and some tender leafy greens. They can easily grab ripe fruits off the trees. They have "hands" to pick, and teeth that can easily rip open a ripe fruit. The length of the intestines and the pH of the stomach acid, shows that it is designed to digest fruits. By all the criteria mentioned, we fall into this last category. We are Frugivores.

If we are all the same on the inside, how come we do not feel good on the same diet? How can it be that what one person thrives on, makes another person ill? Well, to me there is only one answer to that question. As we are all the same in the making, we are only different through our weaknesses. So, what that means is we can only be as alike as how well our bodies are functioning.

As long as a body is clean and functioning as it should, it will thrive on the foods that it was made to consume. The great part is that any weakness can be balanced, and any so called genetic ancestry, can be rewritten. Yes, we can rewrite our DNA!

What most humans are consuming today is very far from being foods from nature. We were not made to consume pesticides, fungicides, additives, carcinogens etc. We were made to eat *food*. All this poison is making us acidic. It is making so many imbalances within our systems that we think we are different from each other. We think we need chemical medicine to function. An animal will only get a human disease when it starts eating human foods. Think about that, the food and health connection is huge! No matter how spiritual we get, it is all energy, and foods are energy also.

When we do not eat up to our potential, we will know it. We all know it. I remember so well all those heavy dinners where you just want to lie down afterwards. Completely drained of energy. Food is supposed to be fuel, not to drain your energy. This only shows that the body has a hard time with what it is being fed. There is no way we can eat what is not good for us and not know it on one level or another. The problem is that we are surrounded with so much toxic waste that our pineal gland is clouded. That makes it harder to connect with our inner wisdom. Once we detoxify our body we will see, think, and perceive everything in a clear and obvious manner.

While on the topic of misinformation and lack of awareness, let me bring up milk, another hot topic. Even though this might not seem as a part of my story, it is. This is a topic that personally held me back my whole life. I am a firm believer, that had it not been for my heavy consumption of these non-human foods, my journey would have been different.

The belief and direct teaching, trough media and trusted authorities is that we need milk from an animal, mostly from cows, to get our calcium. Do we really need to drink breast milk created for a calf, to get the calcium that the mother cow made from grass? *And* do we need to keep drinking it, to keep healthy, like every other animal does *not?* Have you ever seen a cow drink milk? Of course not! They get their calcium from the greens, like we were also intended to. We are made to eat fruits and greens. We will thrive on what we were designed to eat, never lacking anything.

We are designed to drink the water from the juicy fruits, and the clean water that was once there. I had gone from literally living on diet coke, drinking half a gallon a day, to drinking water and fresh juices only. My coffee and beer became a faded memory as my body responded to the living substances of creation.

The very first thing I changed when I got the stool test back showing massive bacterial overgrowth, was the water I was drinking. On any health regimen, or protocol, the water one drinks will be a topic. I had been drinking regular Norwegian tap water my whole life, on top of the not so good well water. I remember when bottled water came to Norway and we were all laughing. We had the best water in the world, the cleanest water, and only stupid people would ever pay money for water. The industry was smart, and not too many years down the road, any Norwegian would gladly pay money for a bottle of water. After my test, I immediately switched from tap to bottled water, thinking that this was going to give me clean, healthy water. Stillwater, that has been sitting in a plastic bottle for God knows how long, will never be healthy water. Neither will tap water from asbestos containing old pipes. Yes, I found that asbestos was present in the water pipes where I had been growing up. Water needs to be clean, and I most definitely see it as a basic human need. The more juicy fruits we eat, and the more hydrated we get, the less water we will need and crave.

My knowledge and trials led me from bottled water, to alkaline ionized water, and finally to distilled water. I found the alkalized, ionized water, through the alkaline lifestyle programs. I drank it for many years, until I was starting to get thrown off by the white mineral coating that was left on my water jugs. I became aware that the inorganic minerals in the water were accumulating in the body. I wanted my minerals from plants, not from rocks. We do not need the inorganic minerals that are present in the soil, but the minerals made organically available for us through the plants. I do not look to my water for any of my nutritional needs, but rather to the fresh living fruits and vegetables. I switched to distilled water about 3 years ago. Pure clean water. Nothing I did not need, only pure H2O. Now, all I drink is fresh juices and distilled water, period. No alcohol, no milk, no soda, no coffee, just pure life-giving elixirs. How sweet it is.

Chapter 16

I am doing this!

My walk had taken so many turns, yet the path was a straight line back to life. There had been so many ups and downs, yet every down was in fact another step forward. When you are riding the wave of healing, everything falls apart. Everything becomes chaos, and from that chaos, in time, comes order. It is like everything that has ever been suppressed or declined will come forth to say hello. The good the bad and the ugly. All persistently letting you know that they mean business.

Before I even knew that I would ever be able to endure- or walk such a walk, I knew that we, all humans, have potentials way beyond what we are conditioned to believe. Our greatest fear is not our weaknesses, but that we are powerful beyond our imagination. Boy are we powerful, ALL of us!

I am honoring my progress:

I am shouting for my husband. I cannot remember the last time I felt this invigorated or ecstatic. I find myself at the top of the stairs, shouting for him to come NOW! "You have to see this, watch me, and get the iPhone! Get up here, get my phone, go down again, and shoot a video of me! Hurry!" *He rushes, believing something must have happened to me. I am smiling:* "Watch me!" *I then walk down the stairs, one foot at the time! I mean, I am walking down one foot at the time, not the way I have been doing it for the last 7 years! I am able to walk regularly down the stairs! I am wearing sneakers, and I feel blessed. Again, I am walking down the stairs! Wow!*

Already I have to be reminded that I needed help to get in and out of a chair not too long ago. I needed to keep my feet elevated constantly. My feet would not reach the floor while seated, for years. They were too inflamed to bend, and now, it is like it happened in a different lifetime. I am already forgetting, wow, I am ecstatic!

Every day I walked in my favorite little forest. Every single day I thanked God for letting me experience this blessing that living is. Every day I enjoyed the fresh air and the freeing sounds of nature. It gave me the inspiration I needed to keep walking and serving. I could vividly remember not being able to walk to the bathroom. I was now walking, using my spinning bike and rebounder. I was on my way, learning how to run again.

From doing what I knew had to be done, looking back to see the enormous shift that had happened for my health on all levels was a pure joy. My rebounding sessions had gone from barely moving, while holding on to the handrail, to jumping full force. We even purchased a large trampoline for the garden, and I am able to jump as much as I like. Let us get out more and play!

From being too anxious to go downstairs, to the mailbox or anywhere else for that matter, I was now completely free of that ghost. My inner feeling of trust and security had taken the place of the uneasiness and fearfulness. I now went to the hairdresser, or any waiting room, without even thinking about how my heart used to pound in my chest in those situations. It is through looking back I truly see the change that has taken place. The subtle changes, most often, are not noticeable until you look back. We forget that the issue was even there. I never thought that I would ever forget, but I do, thankfully we do.

I still have to be reminded of my 15 plus years of stomach pain and indigestion. My husband looked at me the other morning saying: "I remember holding my hand on your stomach for healing every day, do you remember? Do you remember that you were always in pain and could not eat anything without it getting worse?" I *do* remember, but it has faded from my conscious life. I was used to lying on the floor at night in pain, drowning the pain with food and alcohol on the weekends. The constipation was rough, and now, I am moving my bowels three times a day. Well, yes, it is true. A healthy bowel moves after every meal. I would never have believed it possible. The process has been a bumpy one, as a weak digestion will have an acidic intestinal lining. It will have mucus that needs to be released, and it will feel each step. I have seen mucus, blood, sulfur and parasites come out me, and if I could do it, anyone can do it. I am happy to report a smiling, flat, pain-free tummy - that agrees with everything that I eat.

There is no more inflamed collarbone, or inflamed jaw. I can open my mouth fully, and my dentist is thrilled. The inflamed gums are all healed, and my teeth are shining white, strong and clean.

My massages have gone from needing a specific what-*not*-to-do-to-me instruction, to full relaxation and no restrictions attached. I couldn't lie on my stomach, and my elbows could not be lifted. I now have full range of motion in my shoulders, and the freedom of fully being able to do my hair if I wish, is back.

I am thrilled to report that my passion for shoes now has new hope. I am the proud owner of a fair amount of shoes that I can wear. It started out by me finding this great shoe blocker. He opened a new world to be, by blocking a few flat winter shoes for me a few years back. I can now wear a variety of shoes, in different styles and shapes. My high heels are still on the shelf though, and might come to play in time. Right now, some of my toes are still bent from all those years of battling inflammation, but they are restoring, little by little. Barefoot is my all-time favorite though, as there is nothing like grounding and connecting with mother earth.

My days of being pushed around a shopping mall in a wheelchair are over. I am out shopping, walking the town streets, and carrying my own groceries. I am feeling the freedom of being special aids free, although that was not the prediction I was given. Little things like driving a car again is precious to me. For several years I could not drive my car. I could not lift my arms, let alone turn the wheel. My feet were not able to use the pedals, and I could not turn my head. Not a good combination. Now, I do not even think twice about driving, If I need to drive, I drive.

I can tolerate both heat and cold again. From not wanting to go outside in the sun because it would make my heart race and give me dizzy spells, I now love the sun and the hot weather. From dreading to walk outside in the snow, because my hands and feet would ache, I now love to walk in the snow, even to take my shoes off and go barefoot on it! I have learned that cold is alkaline and heat is acidic.

I am wearing slim fit pants, and my knees are shining, inflammation-free and happy! The swollen unbendable knees are history. After being swollen, even after surgery, and after five years of hard work, they gave in. I am very proud of my knees, and they will never have to face being replaced. I love my knees, they are keepers.

Remember my first three-hour car-ride, lying down? A memory that feels like a different lifetime. My life has shifted from night to day. The first trip to California, the helplessness and the despair. The fear and the pain, almost impossible to fully recall. The trips to Florida, with a wheel chair, spending most of the time in bed or on a sunbed. Then, finding our own place in Florida, connecting with like-minded people and finding community.

A year ago, the ultimate accomplishment was me travelling to Florida all by myself! Yes, all by myself! I had set myself free, and I will never forget the feeling of being alone, *knowing* that I was ok, that my life was back, and that I was strong. I could feel the strength and the power of health shining through. From needing help with everything, I now travel, drive around, go shopping, pack up for the beach, swim in the ocean and send out a thank you for every breath I take.

My life has become my passion, and living is the gift that keeps on giving. I have been hosting raw food seminars and given public talks. I have been able to use my education and my experiences to help others, and I am humbly aware of the blessing and responsibility that is.

The unexpected detour:

I was really ok now. My joints were still healing, but I was ok. I had my life back, and I was free to play and create, with my physical body. Then, something happened that made my experience take a completely different turn. I was totally taken by surprise, and I could not believe this was happening to me. I was in shock, to say the least!

"I love getting massages, and I know this one is going to be special. I have met an amazing woman online, Zoe, who is visiting my home town for the weekend. She is a massage therapist and a healer. As soon as I see her I feel her energy, a healing, mild and generous energy. As I lay down on the massage table in the basement of the home of a friend of hers, I feel like I am floating. She is massaging my back, and every time she moves her hands up my spine, I hear the words freedom, freedom, freedom. My whole body is tingling. I am on my back now, and as I feel her touching my arms, I see these amazing white wings growing. They are huge! They are growing until I can no longer see the end of them. I keep feeling an enormous sense of freedom. I am free, it keeps ringing in my ears. Freedom!

I loved the massage and I love her, my new found soul sister. I am ready to leave, feeling great in my new sneakers, yes, me, walking in my sneakers! I gather my things, as I always bring my own oil that I make it from organic jojoba oil and essential oils. So, I am carrying my oil, a few incent things that I was gifted, and my jacket. When I reach the hallway, I realize I have forgotten my car keys.

My friend is calling out to me; "Are you ok, how do you feel?" I feel like I am on top of the World. "I feel fantastic!" I answer loud and clear. In that same moment, as I turn to get my keys, the rug feels like it is literally pulled from underneath me. I lift my feet to protect my knees. (I am very protective of them after everything they have been through). My hands are full, carrying everything, so I am literally shooting out my left hip, hitting the stone floor head on, or hip on rather. What a long second in time. It feels like I am flying in slow motion. I am on the floor, I cannot get up, something is very wrong. The pain is indescribable. I am trying to figure out how to move, how to change the position that I am in. My friend is yelling; "Are you ok?" No, I am not ok! She comes running. My whole leg is pointing inwards, in a freaky direction, and my hip bone is too visible. I am sure it is dislocated. That must be it. The upstairs friend and her husband are there now, and a pillow is put underneath my head.

"Call the ambulance," *I whisper.* "Something is very wrong with my foot." *There is no position for me to hold it in, the pain is too much. Oh my God, are you kidding me? This must be a joke, I mean, really? I have to get my son. I am supposed to pick up Thomas on my way home. I whisper to the people around me;* "Call Thomas, and call Helge, my husband. Find the numbers on my cell, look for Helge`s number is on my cell-phone. Let me talk to him, I can do this." *I need to tell him to bring my stuff to the hospital and meet me there. I register a phone being held to my ear;* "Bring me some juices and my oils, and I might not get out tonight." *I put down the phone, my heart is racing. I focus on my breathing, while I am holding on to Zoe`s warm comforting hand.*

The ambulance is finally here. I am presented with a needle, and I react instantly. What are they going to do? "You need this for the pain," *I am told by the man in the bright uniform, and I really do!* "I am very clean," *I mumble,* "I have not taken an aspirin even, in 7 years, and I only put clean organic food into my system. You have to give me a baby dosage."

I am positive that a full dose of Valium will kill me, for sure. The man is very understanding, and baby dose by baby dose he is able to give me enough to have me moved. Strapped and covered, I am taken to the ambulance, and my new friend comes with me, never letting go of my hand. This whole time she is speaking to me, telling me how everything is great, and that I am doing good. Like an angel she stands beside my bed in the ER, while the surgeon rushes to meet me. After doing the routine x-rays, I see the same surgeon again. He is serious when he looks at me. "It is not out of place, is it, dislocated…" *I try.* "No, it is not. It is broken right off, it is the hip bone, and you need surgery right now. This is a bad fracture I am afraid." *He gives me a compassionate look. I feel empty. Ok, so I am really experiencing this. I keep breathing.*

My husband is here, and he has brought my son and my daughter. Thomas is on his way to Oslo, so quite a hectic good bye. This is out of my control, and I am just drifting at this point. I am taken to surgery, and that is all that I know. I have to let go.

I wake up, greeted by this beautiful woman in a white uniform. She has a big smile on her face; "You are amazing", she says. "And you look radiant". I am? I do? "Yes, here is my e-mail address, I want you to contact me, your story and your lifestyle is fascinating. I have never met anyone like you."

I am stumbled. Have I been going on without even knowing it? I have been talking away without being fully awake? Oh well, it must be real passion. Crazy. I give the woman my e-mail address, and thank her for her kind words. I lie in this calm energy, until someone comes for me.

I am wheeled to my room shared by 5 others. My husband is waiting. He looks serious. I am fine. My juice is already on my night stand. I am good. I can do this. I will recover. This is what I am thinking, I am a bit confused, but I am here now, and I need to sleep.

The surgeon comes to see me, Dr. Sola, and he shows me a picture. I can keep it. Wow, I had no idea they could even do that! I have plates, bolts and screws in me, the picture shows. Not my favorite thing, to have a leg and hip filled with metals, but it was done, and I am told it is in for life. I am grateful for this man. My leg was pointing in the wrong direction, and the surgeon had worked hard to mend me back together. The healing is expected to take around a year to full recovery, and the first three months will be in bed. I can use a walker back and forth to the bathroom after 6 weeks, but no putting any weight on the foot until the 3-month mark. I am in shock, really? I just got back to walking, and now this? Ok, I can do that. I will keep doing my thing, and it will be fine.

A new doctor is at my bedside now, telling me I lost a lot of blood during the operation.

"You need blood transfusion. You also have too little protein in your blood, and your body will not be able to heal very well. Your scar will have troubles healing at all." *He says.*

He is looking at me like I am a foreigner. I do not want blood. I agree that if the blood count is not pointing upwards by the next day, I will take his advice. The Doctor is on-board. We will check again the next morning. I am praying.

The pain medications and the anesthesia has made me very unwell. My body is crying for relief, and I decide there will be no more drugs. I am sure the pain after the surgery is manageable somehow, and if not, well, I can always reconsider. I cannot move my leg at all, it is swollen from heel to hip. I have been on a stretcher I am told. They had to relocate my whole leg to drill it back in place. All I can do is to lie still on my back, and breathe. The nighttime is the worst. The hospital sounds and noises are so unfamiliar and loud. Five other people are sleeping in the same room, medication-time in the middle of the night, and lights go on and off.

I am uneasy, and a nurse stops by my bed. She raises her voice; "So, you are not feeling well, are you? Shows you to do as the doctor tells you and get that blood infusion, doesn't it, I hope you regret that now. Next time you better do as you are told!" *Am I dreaming? Is this woman saying this to me? She is. I say nothing. Who told her about the blood transfusion, and what an odd thing to say. I try to sleep.*

It is morning, and I am visited bedside by a nutritionist. He is telling me I need to eat more protein. He has seen on my chart that I am a vegan, that I am not eating any animal protein. I nod, that is correct. He is young but confident; "You need to eat more protein, or you will never heal", *he continues. I nod again. I do not have any energy to spend on the topic, and decide to let it rest. I am confident, and I know that I am feeding my body what it needs. That is all I need to know, and that is all I need to care about. I am in pain, and I need to rest.*

The doctor from the day before is happy. The blood count has already started to rise, so I am off the hook. "You will be fine", *he says, no transfusion needed. He tells me that coming in, I had had an iron/hemoglobin count that was very high. I have not seen that high a number since way before I was diagnosed. I have been anemic for years! Wow, this is great news for me! It shows that the inflammation in the body really was kicked to the curb. I hang on to that, as I feel a fever come on. I am shivering, nauseated and I feel weak and tired.*

Someone pokes me; "Time to get up!" *I open my eyes, trying to focus on the voice;* "Time to get out of bed!" *I see three women in white standing by my bed. They have brought a walker. I tell them that I have a fever, feel like I am going to throw up, and that they will have to come back later.* "No, you are going to get out of bed now, you need to start moving around." *One of them boldly states.* "I will try later, but right now, there is no way I can get up. I am feeling dizzy and anxious," *I try. I am then grabbed by my shoulders and hands. All three of them lifting me up to an upright position. My head is hanging and I feel faint.* "Please," *I say,* "I cannot do this right now, I feel sick. My foot has a throbbing pain, and my back feels like it has been ripped in two!" *Rejection not noted. I am lifted out of the bed to a standing position, and my leg feels like it is being torn off me. I am hanging on to the walker. I am hanging by my elbows. One woman is in front of me wheeling the thing, one is on the side, and on is behind me. We are on our way down the hallway. I keep stating that I do not feel well, this is not right, it is not a good thing! I must be in the Twilight zone. I look down, and I see that I am leaving a trail of blood behind me, and my wound is oozing.*

Back in bed, a nurse comes to change the bandage on my leg. It is still bleeding and oozing liquid. "This is because you lack protein, she says." "Ok," *I answer. I am definitely NOT up for a chat on any subject today. I need to get out of here, that is what is dawning on me.*

The other patients in my room are talking. They do not like that I am on a different diet, the no-thank-you diet as far as they are concerned. I can hear them saying that we should all be thankful for what is given to us. I agree with that 100%, we should be, and I am. I am very grateful for everything given to me, and most of all my choice to do what is best for me, like drinking my juices and eating my real food.

That afternoon, I am moved to a different room. I am alone now, what a blessing. I finally get in contact with my husband and my best friend May. They are in shock after hearing what I have been experiencing. My fever is rising, and I am not feeling comfortable here. I cannot move my foot, but being medication-free is fine. The pain is manageable, and this way I can feel what is going on in my body. It has already started to detoxify the drugs from my system, and I am going to let it. I do not need this shit. I want to go home. I need to go home. My health is depending on it.

The hospital agrees to release me the next day. All I want is my own bed, my fruits, juices and some peace and quiet. This is no healing environment. This is no place to rest and recuperate. Not for me, not for anyone. I need flowers and fresh air, and I need some hugs. A lot of hugs! My husband is on it. When can I get out? Later today, I am told. A nurse drops by to tell me the news; "Let your husband pick you up when he can this afternoon". Pick me up? As in me sitting in a regular car? I cannot even sit up by myself, let alone get out of a bed, get up the stairs to my bed, or do anything besides lie flat on my back. She is actually telling me he should come pick me up? This must be a joke, but I am not laughing. My fever is still high, but I say nothing. I call my husband again. He is furious at this time. He calls the hospital to arrange my transportation home, and this is what he is told. "We are not sending her home in an ambulance, as she can get in the car fine. She was up walking yesterday!"

I think this is where my hubby changed his gear big time. They are telling him I had been up, walking around! They are telling him that me hanging from the walker, un-willingly supported and dragged by the helpers from Cruel-City was me up walking? Within a few hours, two amazing men are lifting me onto a stroller, driving me home in an ambulance. My spirit is lifted. I can heal now. We did it!

I am well back in the second floor of my home, accompanied by bandages and tin buckets. Now I can go to the bathroom in my bed. Just dandy. I know this is what is needed. I do not care, I am too sick to care, no trips to the bathroom is fine for now.

The next week is detox-week from hell. I am throwing up and having almost non-stop diarrhea. The headache is constant, and I still have a low grade fever. Then, all of a sudden, it is done. My body is done, and everything is out, it is over. I am in awe, feeling my strength coming back, and I am ready to get to what I need to do. I have some serious training and healing to do on top of my usual protocol. I am back in bed, but this time, not for long.

The smaller community where I live has put me on this amazing program. They are sending over a nurse, a physical therapist, and other helpers, so that I am not in lack of anything. They are carrying food from the downstairs kitchen to my upstairs bed two times a day, helping me wash up, bringing hot water and towels. Walkers, and a toilet for my bedroom, all taken care of. I mean, I am amazed of these fantastic helpers. There is nothing they will not do for me. I would have been lost without them. My walking down the stairs period is put on hold. Upstairs living is here again.

The hugs that I wished for are coming in, in abundance, and the visitors and flowers are many. I am back online, and can continue my passion and joy. My hemoglobin is rising fast, and I keep spraying my wound with my essential oil blend. I made my own magical healing oil. I move my foot as often as I can, and I am feeling amazingly little pain after only a few weeks. My body is not letting me down, oh no, it is working like a trooper to balance this trauma. My physiotherapist is happy, and

I am happy. The healing is way beyond her or anyone's expectations. The stitches are out, and after three weeks the scar is already fading! I keep healing, and after two months, I take my first small walk outside again. No animal protein and all!"

Control and X-ray at the hospital after 3 months concludes exceptionally rapid healing. The surgeon just stared at me while I did my stretching and bending act. He never saw anything like it, he says. There is no mentioning of any lack of protein. I am interested in one thing now: Can we remove the steal, ever? Well, it is not what is normally done, but it *is* possible. That is all I need to hear. I am still on a mission, and it will come out.

NOTE: The oil blend recipe is in my book *Know the Truth and get Healthy.*

Chapter 17

Detoxification, the simple key.

O ver the years, I have experienced symptoms I did not even know existed. I had no idea that when I was asking for complete healing I was going to get it on a cellular level. My body was going to get rid of every weak cell no matter where it was in the body, and it was going to push out every toxin stored, in any way that it could. The body that I had been abusing for so many years, the one with the weak kidney and adrenals, the weak skin and stomach, was going to take out the garbage. Let me give you a very brief introduction of what detoxification is, and my own experience and symptoms;

I am sitting in my sauna with my feet up the wall in front of me. I am looking straight at my feet, OMG, my toenails are falling off! I mean, my nails are turning blue! Not that I do not look at my own feet, but this I had not noticed. They are loose! I have experienced too much to freak out, but this is by far my most extreme symptom. Wow, so my body wants new nails, huh? I can only shake my head and smile, as I shift my focus to something else.

Three nails fell off, grew back beautifully, and that was that. More on my symptoms later. I want to introduce you to the art of detoxification, the understanding of health and healing.

There is no magic bullet to great health. There is no quick fix, no pill or supplement that will take you from suffering to thriving. There is no product of any kind that will restore health in an unbalanced, diseased body. *Only* the body can do any healing, any balancing, and any regeneration. Again, only the body can do the healing, it is a self-healing mechanism. That is what it does, it does anything in its power to stay healthy, to regenerate. Think of what happens when we cut ourselves - we heal. The body rushes to stop the bleeding, and to regenerate. We tend to confuse symptom suppression with true healing.

Detoxification is a word we use when we talk about cleansing. It is a word often used, and it has many meanings and connotations.

Detoxification simply means cleansing, and the body does that around the clock. It needs to cleanse to survive.

Why does the body need to cleanse? Well, the body is made of more than a hundred trillion cells, for the sake of a number, and they all *eat*, and they all *poop*. The poop is what we call cellular waste. Every cell generates waste, and on top of that, what we eat, breathe and live, generates waste. In the same way that we are brushing our teeth and taking a shower, ever cell and every organ needs to cleanse and clean itself on an ongoing basis. When we are experiencing symptoms of less than optimal health, the body is showing us that our elimination of waste is not functioning as it should. The lymphatic system is now stagnant, and the acidic waste is burning our cells. Again, look at the lymph system as the sewer system of the body. It is where all the waste is dumped to be carried to the different elimination organs. The blood needs to be clean, as it is the kitchen, the carrier of nutrition, oxygen and all vital components for a healthy cell. All we are is cells, more than a trillion of them. That is a lot of *poop!*

Here we are, with all this waste that is supposed to naturally leave the body.
Here we are with all the symptoms of a body full of acids, full of poop and sewage that is making us sick.
Here we are, making ourselves sick, not even knowing about it most of the time.
Here we are resorting to more poisons to feel better, by taking drugs and stimulants.

So the blood is the kitchen, bringing in the food to feed the cells. More for the cells to eat, and more waste is created. This simple idea is to awaken us to the fact that it is through proper detoxification, by moving the lymph, eliminating cellular and metabolic waste, that true regeneration, alkalization and hydration can happen.

So you see, on top of waste naturally created in the body every minute just from living, the diet of the modern world includes more waste. Food is not supposed to be waste, but sadly it is. Chemicals, GMO, cooked and altered, filled with more damaging substances than I even care to focus on, are poisoning our bodies every day. The kidneys are especially impaired by the ingestion of animal protein. So much metabolic waste comes from trying to break down the protein, that the kidneys get really tired and weak. Through the weakening of our most important elimination organ, the kidneys, the lymph system is unable to properly filter out the acidic, the metabolic and the dietary waste. Along with the intestines, the liver, the lungs, and the skin, the kidneys are on a mission to keep you healthy in every way possible.

School is in session: The body is always working *for* you, and never against you.

173

To regain health, to strengthen the whole body, to thrive and live free of pain and suffering, the body needs to be clean. It needs to be running smoothly in every way. It needs to get rid of what is obstructing the flow of life. When we talk about detoxification, we are talking about letting the body do what it was designed to do. We are simply talking about getting out of the way, about stopping what is hurting it. We are stopping what is creating more waste, so that the body can use its energy to cleanse.

As time goes by, it becomes harder to feel good in our home, the body, as clutter and garbage will be obstructing the energies and the peace. The air will be hard to breathe, so to speak, and the different equipment within will no longer function optimally. Our body is our temple, and where we spend all our time in this lifetime. It is a permanent residency, and that is an absolute. The lymph system is the body's sewer system, and to carry out the waste, it needs to be moving and disposing of the garbage.

It is natural to be healthy, and the body is working in that direction every single minute!

Detoxification is not only about food though, on the contrary - it is about letting everything that is not serving us be processed and leave. A true healing regime or program will include emotional and mental work also. It will be impossible not to include this important work. The mind, body and soul connection again. Never the less, changing what we eat most often is the simplest and most potent way to start. The body will detoxify all our bodies at the same time; The physical, the mental and the emotional body. That means that once we start to eat what the body is designed to eat, it will also let us know which emotional waste we have been holding on to. By giving it a break from having to digest and eliminate more waste, it now has the ability to use the energy to clear everything from old emotions to mucus in our intestines.

All you have to do is to let go of everything that is not serving you, be it foods, emotions or actions. The body will do the rest!

We are sick and tired, and sick and tired of being sick and tired. I was very sick and tired of being sick and tired, and I have finally found the road back. The path from Hell to Inspired is now crystal clear to me. What was making me sick, had to come out. Health had to be able to shine through and take charge! We need to look to nature, get back to the basics, and trust in our own bodies and their ability to heal. We will heal by eating fresh living organic foods, like we were meant to eat. That way, we are constantly letting our body take care of business. In this lifetime, in this world, the challenges are many for most of us. It seems the non-foods presented to us, alongside the stress, the polluted air, the negative programming and the fear of change, is holding us captive in our polluted houses.

I was cleaning out my house, and letting the fresh air in. I was taking charge of my home, knowing from my core that I am the only one responsible for how it feels, looks and functions. Simplicity had hit me big time. Stop bringing in more garbage. Move the lymph. Open all eliminating organs. Let the sun shine in.

Everyone will experience different detoxification symptoms. They are a reflection of the health and strength of the elimination organs, the glands, the weaknesses and the general energy level of the body. The symptoms will also tend to feel the strongest where you are the weakest. Not all symptoms while healing, are detoxification symptoms. Some are healing symptoms. That means that when the body starts to heal an old wound, it might feel painful all over again. You will feel the body healing what it was not able to fully heal the first time around. The healing might simply have been suppressed with medications. When the body is given the chance to clean its house, it will do so, and once the cleaning is done, it will go on repairing and rebuilding. So, cleaning first, then repair and rebuild.

Typical symptoms of the body loosening up old mucus and transporting out old waste, is the release of mucus. It can be new mucus, made to carry out bacteria or toxins, or it can be older mucus that the body has been holding on to for years. It can look like what we call cold and flu like symptoms. Any opening can be used for excreting toxins from the body, so the nose, the throat, our colon, our ears, the kidneys, and the eyes, all available for the body to use. Next time you need to blow your nose, celebrate! Your body is doing its job, expelling mucus!

The body can also raise the temperature to get rid of bacteria and microbes, so a low grade fever is a common detoxification symptom. Other common symptoms of the cleansing mechanism are headaches, dizziness, rashes and itching, fatigue and hair loss, and more!

The body will get to work on any weak or damaged part of the body. Even an old scar will fade over time. Only healthy cells will be left, and any weak cell will have to go. The whole point is to let the body get rid of everything that is weakened and damaged, and it will. It is so eager to do so, that it jumps to the task the minute it gets a chance.

The symptoms of healing from detoxification:

My detoxification symptoms have been many, ranging from mild to severe. For years and years, I have been having symptoms of my body's healing and cleansing. I am sure we will have periods of cleansing on and off for the rest of our lives, as long as we eat clean and live free. The body will eventually obtain the ability to cleanse on an ongoing basis, like it is designed to.

I have experienced everything from rashes to blisters, hives and boils. There was so much mucus residing under my skin, I was ready to burst. My skin was always clear though, so little did I know that my skin was in trouble. As I started to detoxify my body, my skin would break out in terrible rashes. Full body itching from hell-rashes. I have had herpes breakouts, lumps on my tongue, and hives that came and went for years. For a whole year my face looked like I had the chicken pox. Pimples, dots, all over my face. Some days less, some days more. Red burning cheeks that were peeling even. The acids were coming out, and it felt like burns. The burning acid.

I have had high fevers, and low grade fevers, whole body pains and general flue like symptoms. For years I felt like I had a hangover but missed the party. The nausea has been constant for long periods of times, and even my newborn perfect digestion has been set on hold for short periods of time. When the stomach and intestines are releasing sulfur, mucus and acids from the walls, you will feel it. I sure did and do. Gas, bloating, acid pain and diarrhea is the name of that game. I have lost nails, and most of my hair. The hair part is probably one of the scariest symptoms that I have experienced. My hair was long, thick and beautiful, and suddenly, it was falling out. Now, that was a freaky symptom! The weak cells had to be released, and my weaknesses were showing themselves. The weaknesses in the body will always come forth when the mask is taken off, so to speak. My head was detoxifying bigtime, and my eyes, my hair, the swollen lips and the bumpy tongue, all symptoms of toxic waste moving in the head, trying to get out.

I've experienced rushes of anxiety and depression. My joints have been swelling and burning, making me wonder if I was healing- or hurting myself. I believe that the toughest symptoms we go through on a healing path are those that look like the symptoms we are trying to heal. When that happens it is easy to get fearful.

I have told you this before, I was one toxic puppy! I am amazed at what this body has been able to do. Even though it was beat down, poisoned and weak, it was able to get the job done. No matter how much I had tried to kill it, it was still able and willing to get back on its feet. I am in awe of what a body can achieve, once we get out of the way. Nature really *is* perfect.

"Dear body. I am so sorry for abusing you during all these years. I am amazed at your ability to heal and regenerate. I will always respect you and be your best friend. I know better now, and we are a team!" -Hilde

Chapter 18

Mind-body-spirit connection

ealing and regeneration will always start with the mind. It will start with a thought, as everything does. If you can think it, imagine it and feel it, you can do it. Everything ever created has been a thought first. The willingness to change, to heal and to grow, is the power that we all hold and can tap in to. The true power of life, lies in the freedom of choice. We might not always be able to choose every event, or so it might seem, but we can always choose our reaction to it. Our response is our own, always.

I recognized that life was so much grander than me, yet at the same time, I was all that is. The humbleness and the gratitude that comes from seeing just how powerful life and healing is, has changed my life completely. I have seen that my every thought, and my every emotion generates a manifestation in my life. I am the one that is holding the key, and I am never a victim of any circumstance. My ill health and my imbalanced life was all cause and effect. It was all a reaction to actions, and so was the reversal and balancing of my whole being.

My weak cells were handed down to me from my parents, and my thought patterns were imprinted in me from my early childhood, and also from past lives. The dietary habits were picked up along the path of life, and the effect was mine to experience. I always knew that the mind was powerful, and I always knew that it held an important piece of my healing puzzle. My general positive attitude and outlook on life made it natural for me to adopt to the importance of thinking health promoting thoughts.

Our mind is constantly talking, constantly telling us how it is. Now, imagine that most of what you're thinking is not even conscious thoughts. The unconscious mind is a tricky friend, that often does *not* work in our favor. The tricky thing is that we cannot know what we are really thinking about, except by analyzing our surroundings. Our lives will tell us what we are thinking about most of the time, because that *is* what we will manifest.

"The subconscious mind controls 95 percent of how our circumstances manifest and our beliefs shape our lives. The power of the subconscious is about a million times greater than our conscious mind."- Bruce Lipton, PhD

My interest for the mind-body-soul connection has been a very passionate one. My experiences during my dreamlike state, my Ayahuasca journey and my meditations, have all shown me that everything is perfectly flowing together. My introduction to Louise Hay, Eckhart Tolle, Deepak Chopra, Bruce Lipton, Dr. Wayne W Dyer, and many more, were reflecting back to me what I knew to be true. I knew that my mind was powerful, and that by altering my thoughts and emotions, I could change the course of my life. I was led to meditations and the teachings of subliminal programming. I had to rewrite my story, and it had to start with my mind, and my subconscious mind most importantly.

"Ask, and it is given" by Jerry and Ester Hicks, the teachings of Abraham, is a powerful book, and it opened my eyes even more. This was truth. To me, there was nothing more freeing than recognizing that I, and only I was responsible for how my life was manifesting. That also meant that the same I, as in *me*, was the one who could change it. I was so *in*, and I was already on the mission of reading anything I could come across on the subject. The movie "The secret" came out at this time, but I could see that to fully grab the concept, one had to get out of the mind, and into the emotional state. The power of feeling good now, is beyond belief.

A great part of any healing process, any eagerness for life and beyond, holds a great deal of humbleness.

I found that life is so much grander than me, and the more I seek to mentally *understand,* the more is revealed to me of what is not to be understood. Like any other species, I see us as a perfect part of nature, with the same ability to heal and regenerate. All we need to do is stop what is making us sick, tired, stressed out, angry, hopeless and helpless, and allow God's greatness. What is the story we have been telling ourselves? Every day, at every moment, a word, a chapter is written. Our life story is told in the way that we live, and how we choose to tell our story will manifest our reality.

On one of my barefoot walks, I really fell into the story of my life. What am I surrounding myself with? What are the words I keep telling myself, and what am I trying to prove to myself and others? True freedom comes from true empowerment, and that is a pretty large statement. What is true empowerment? Well, to me it is the ability to stay true to oneself at all times.

- *To be able to choose to live authentically and to love and cherish one self.*

- *To be able to feel the freedom that comes from abandoning the concept of having to follow the crowd, in order to find happiness.*

- *To be able to choose health, friends, actions and attitude.*

- *To feel proud of who we are and what we have accomplished.*

We need to declare our story, and walk our talk. Then, we will set ourselves free from anything that is holding back our beautiful spirit from fully expressing itself!

Feeling good generates more to feel good about.

The practice of meditation is a powerful tool. It will still the mind and help us tap into the now-moment, which holds everything. I meditated for one hour every single day for many years. I kept using the subliminal reprogramming audios, but also pure and simple stillness. Connecting with my breath, sitting, letting the mind rest, is all that you need. At first, it was hard to not get lost in all the thoughts that were popping into my head. I was an over-thinker, believe me. I had what is called a "monkey mind" - it just never seemed to shut up! No matter what, it was talking away, so for me, practicing meditation and stillness was a must. I needed to train myself to be silent. My inner state was so clearly reflecting my outer busy, high adrenalin, uneasy life. I recognized that I had to start with my inner world, and the outer would follow. Easy? Not at all!

Day by day I was getting better at it, and I was able to connect more and more with the stillness and the messages that my body was sending me. I was lead to raw foods, nature, and was shown that the mind is a simple tool, and that love and compassion is the true power of creation. The more I practiced, the humbler I got. From sitting in stillness, my practice has now changed to being aware when I am out in nature. I find that walking outside *is* my meditation. It is my time of being in the now. I don`t focus so much on stillness anymore, but rather on being a receiver. I am listening, open to receive anything that will benefit me.

"Show me the way, how can I serve, thank you for this healing."

I can see that my journey has woven all parts of my being together like a perfectly knitted blanket. I was introduced to meditation, to the God force and the divine creation, while learning the powerful effect of the affirming mind. The focus of the mind, through vision boards and affirmations was as important as eating clean foods, breathing clean air, and drinking pure water. The willingness to heal, the mental focus, the conditioned mind and the pure intent was all interwoven in the creation of life. There is no separation, and we are the ones responsible for untangling the knots. I had no idea how to get to the knots or how many there were, but I knew early on that they were mine, and that I was the one that had to untangle them.

Affirmations can be tricky. When we are very sick, and keep telling ourselves "I am perfectly healthy", our mind is not going to believe us, obviously. The gap between what is the current experience and the statement is too big. I kept telling myself that I was healthy, but clearly I was not. The "feeling better and better" statement, using the feelings as a climbing ladder, became a much more natural approach for me.

I was constantly telling myself something like this:

I am feeling better and better every day.
Today is a better day than yesterday.
I am eager about the future, and I am grateful for this amazing experience.
My health is always improving, and I am setting myself free.
I love my life, and I know that it loves me.

I am healthier now than in a very long time, every day, I am getting better.
I am happy.
I know that deep down I am healthy, I am.
Health is natural for me, and I am worthy.
I am worthy of health, and I am living it.

I could believe those words, and they lifted me.

Any affirmation is simply words that are used to generate a feeling. The feeling holds the power of movement of energy. It is the language of the Universe. Visualization is such a powerful tool because it easily draws in the feelings. If you can see it, smell it, and touch it, you can really feel it! Once the feeling is generated, the power of manifestation is set in motion. The ride is ours alone, we make the bed, we lay in it.

I noticed that the cleaner I ate and the more raw-organic foods I consumed, the clearer my mind became. I also noticed that my spiritual connection became stronger. I was able to think clearer, feel stronger and be more balanced. I was able to observe my life from a detached position. What I mean about that, is that instead of being *in* every situation, emotionally attached, driven by drama and emotional ups and downs, I was more and more able to detach myself. The drama around me was no longer mine to take in. I did no longer find myself engaging in any news or gossip. The television is now switched off at our house, and besides my husband watching an occasional game, it is no longer feeding us any drama.

Leaving the old programming and conditioning will lead to detachment from the news and propaganda. Be ready to break free, because once you know, you *know*, and you can never go back to not knowing. You can try, and many do. I was trying for all those years to ignore the signals from my own body, but it kept on knocking on my door until I opened it. After discovering the true power of *me*, there was no turning back. I could no longer choose my diet, it was chosen for me, by the real me. I was guided on a soul level, by my spirit, by God. I was experiencing the inner battle going on inside my body, in my mind, and even in the memories of my cells. Did you know that every cell holds memory? Oh yes, and they hand it down to the new cells. Breaking the cycle is not that hard to do, but one must have the intent and the willingness to do so. When you really know what is hurting you, it is harder and harder to keep doing it.

Health is easy, change is hard.

The more I connected physically with nature, the more I would notice the little messages it was leaving for me. My mind was always clearer during my walks, and my inner conversation changed. From chattering and blabbering away, I was starting to receive what I perceive as clear messages from spirit. I would ask for guidance, and I would get it, instantly! Everything is instant, and I never doubt what I am being told. My eyes are always open when I walk, and I try to stay as much in the *now* moment as I can. I have found that this has become my true meditation. My walks allow me to stay in a state of awareness, and that is what I see as the true connection and the reason for practicing meditation. I talk to the creator and I connect with my higher self. Any way you want to look at it. I connect directly to the source. Being able to look inwards for guidance has been one of the most profound shifts during these years. Even though I never did have much need of authority, I was still seeking approval. My whole life I was seeking to please and perform. I was eager to do good by others, I felt it was expected of me.

The more we talk to the source, and connect with who we really are, the more we will love ourselves. Ultimately everything we are searching for, is rooted in that one thing, loving ourselves. Self-love will resolve any obstruction. Self-love, so simple, yet so hard. We are not told, or even shown, that loving ourselves is the same as loving

God and creation. We are not separable from anything around us, and by not loving ourselves we cannot fully love anything else. By not loving ourselves we stay in a state of self-abuse, and from that comes suffering.

I also connect with nature through the amazing crystals. They are transformational examples of nature. I have a few that are particularly sacred to me. Crystals and gemstones are living formations that have been growing on our earth since the beginning of time. They are considered highly sacred and powerful, and have been used since the dawn of ancient civilization. These ancient crystals are told to have been used by the Lemurian civilization more than 30,000 years ago. Like then, they are now used as aids in physical, emotional and spiritual healing. They are also used for spirit contact and psychic development. My favorite crystal is a clear quartz, but for you it might be a different one. Once you explore them, hold them in your hand, and feel them, you will know. You will know which one is for you. I found crystals to be fun and interesting to learn more about, and the more I learn, the more I feel connected to them. I have been granted the pleasure to lie on John of Gods crystal bed numerous times, and I have been blown away by the power of the crystals and the work of the entities.

When we are working with crystals, we are embarking on a journey of rediscovering and healing of our true, inner self.

It is impossible to write about the mind-body-spirit connection, without mentioning the much inspirational philosophy of Ho'oponopono. This is the optimal recognition of self-responsibility, and acknowledgement of everything that manifests in one's life. A true honoring of every aspect of the mind-body-spirit connection. After reading the story, I was amused.

The therapist Dr. Ihaleakala Hew Len, used an ancient Hawaiian philosophy to cure a complete ward of criminally insane patients.

What is most special about this story is that the man never saw any of the patients in person. He did not have any contact with any of them. The psychologist studied each patient, their charts, and went within himself. He was looking to see how he himself created the person's illness. He found that as he improved himself, the patients improved! This was more than I had thought possible, and went beyond the typical mind- body understanding, that we are powerful in creating our own reality. This story was revealing a much deeper connection. Did we have a way to impact absolutely everything within our experience?

This Hawaiian therapist, in healing those mentally ill people, was teaching us an advanced perspective on taking total responsibility. I mean, he was taking responsibility for everything that crossed his path.

He worked at the Hawaii State Hospital for four years. The ward he was working at, is where they kept the criminally insane and very dangerous patients. It was hard to keep the psychologists employed; They quit or called in sick, as the job was a heavy burden. The story says that people would walk through that ward with their backs against the wall, always afraid of being attacked by patients. To live in, work at, or visit such a place, was a challenge for everyone involved. Dr. Len never saw any patients. He agreed to have an office on site though, so that he could review their files. While he looked at the files, he kept working on himself. Then, as he worked on himself, the patients began to heal.

"Ho'oponopono" is defined in the Hawaiian Dictionary as mental cleansing and setting things right through mutual restitution and forgiveness.

Just months after Dr. Len had started his work, the patients started to show signs of healing. The heavily medicated ones were getting off their medications. The patients that previously had to be contained, were allowed to move around freely. Those who had no chance of ever being released, were being freed. The staff wanted to come back to work, and now, that ward does not exist anymore. This is a true story!

When asked what he was doing with himself, Dr. Len answers: "I was simply healing the part of me that created them."

The philosophy recognizes that your responsibility is with everything you are experiencing in your life. You have to take responsibility for all of it. This is a tough one. In this world, with so much pain and suffering, we are responsible for all of it? According to Ho'oponopono, this means that anything you experience and do not like is there for you to heal. It is all from inside you. The problem is not with them, it is with you, and to change them, you have to change you. Powerful words!

Dr. Hew Len says that Ho'oponopono is a process where we say to The Divine: "I love you" (unification), "I'm sorry" (repentance); "Please forgive me" (forgiveness); and "Thank You" (transmutation).

The practice is simple, according to Dr. Len, *"Just keep saying, I am sorry and I love you over and over again."* That is all. Loving yourself *is* the greatest way to improve yourself, and as you improve yourself, you improve your world. The idea is that we are the sum of our experiences, and that everything we experience is actually a memory, driven from our emotions and which are tied to them. The purpose of Ho'oponopono is to connect with the divine within on a moment-to-moment basis, to ask that movement and all it contains, be cleansed. Only the divine/God can do that. The philosophy acknowledges that only God can erase or correct memories and thought-forms. Since God created us, only God knows what is going on with us.

Love is unconditional, it is a vibration. It is the energy that heals and regenerates every cell. It is on the alkaline side of chemistry true healing takes place. Fresh living fruits and vegetables, sunshine, clean water, nature's vibration, laughter and prayers, are all part of that love for life.

If you want to read more about Dr. Len and Ho'oponopono, I recommend reading the book "Zero Limits" by Dr. Joe Vitale and Dr. Hew Len.

True love is self-love.

A few years ago, I had an experience that I want to share with you. I was lying in my bed, to rest and to meditate, it is late in the afternoon, but not yet night. Sometimes I re-center myself by lying down for some re-connective breathing. This is my experience:

I am lying on a bed, and I can clearly see the end of it. It has a brass or gold like frame. The room seems to be missing a roof, and I am stunned at the fresh air that is breezing through the sheets. I think I am covered by sheets - it feels like it. It is dark, as the sky is dark, but the bed is lit up. Not from a lamp, it is just lit up. I can see my feet, and at the end of the bed stands a woman. She is middle aged and is wearing something that looks like an apron. Her whole outfit is old fashioned and colorless. She has long gray hair, and is looking straight at me. How did I get here? She reaches out her arms, lifts them over my feet and holds them there. "Are you a healer also?" I ask. In that very instant her hands shoot up in the air. The sound is almost unbearably loud, and it is embracing my whole being. A strong wind, like a tornado is blowing through me. As I look at her again, she dissolves into little particles and I shoot out of my body. It happens in the same instant, together with a loud sound.

Then, I am floating, silently and calmly in an infinite place of darkness and light at the same time. I am experiencing a feeling of relief, of bliss and of wonder. "Wow, is this what being without a body feels like?"

Just as I think that thought, using my mind, I am back. I am back in my body".

We are not our bodies. We are souls using the body as a vehicle. It is our responsibility to take care of this vehicle, this house, to be able to experience the best life possible on this earth. We are merely travelers, on a journey, together, yet alone.

PART FOUR

THE POWER WITHIN

Chapter 19

Nature is perfect.

Together with my love for nature, my passion for grounding is deeply rooted. Honoring nature changes everything. It takes us from the mind-game to the heart felt natural way of existence. On my walk and journey, I found that being grounded was very important and profound. I studied grounding sheets and mats, and I even slept on a grounding sheet for years. I have my house full of orgonite, and I have shielded my computers and telephone with EMF protectors. I have consciously done what I have found best to let me live in this crazy electromagnetic noise, with the least amount of negative impact. *But*, and this is a huge but; There is nothing that will do what nature does for us. There is nothing that will reset our cells and clear our energies as a barefoot walk and a tree hug will, so get ready to lose your shoes and socks!

As I'm going about my day, I notice my inner conversation. Did you know that we are talking to ourselves most of the time, every day of the week? We are blabbering along without even noticing. We are constantly talking to ourselves, and the funny thing is, we are mostly *telling ourselves the same thing over and over again. Our mind is like a broken record. I don`t mean that we are telling ourselves to find the car keys over and over again, but we might be thinking about the same things that burden us and makes us stressed or frustrated. We might have a habit of thinking about who did us wrong, how we do not like this and that, or how we no longer love our house.*

So, as I am walking outside, I am really noticing my inner conversation. The woods are quiet, a few birds are singing, no wind, a few cars in the distance, and I am saying: "Thank you, thank you, thank you," over and over again. For the last few years, I have been conditioning myself by repeating, consciously, a few simple sentences:

Thank you for this healing,
how can I serve,
show me the way.

It has been my way of reprogramming my conscious and unconscious mind, to keep its focus on what matters the most to me. Not only what matters the most, but also what I believe will benefit my life and the life of everyone I encounter.

Today, it is simplified to a simple thank you!

What I had been saying to myself for a long time was no longer playing in my head. Thank you was all that was repeating itself to me, showing me the true essence. Words are energy, and they all hold a frequency, an intent and a passion.

Words are submissions of intent, and even when we are not aware, we are sending out a message to our cells, to the creation, to God.

The energy of gratitude is a pure love energy. It is the vibration of constant positive change. Whenever we find ourselves wanting something to change, we must start by being grateful for what we already have. There is always something to be grateful for. Even when we are down, feeling lost and depressed, we can search for that feeling of gratitude. *Being* grateful is the same as ordering more to be grateful for. If we want our health to change, we must be grateful for the work that the body is already doing. Feeling gratitude for our breath, our vision, our hearing etc. If we want a better house to live in, we must be grateful for the home that we already have, or the couch that we are offered by a friend. No matter the status of our current shelter - giving thanks for what is already there, is inviting in more to feel grateful for.

The challenge is that gratefulness does not come from the mind. Gratitude is not a thought, it is a feeling, a state of being. It is a heartfelt feeling and it fills the entire body with nurturing, positive, healing energy. It is very similar to love, but it is directed towards the recognition of all that is. We can be grateful for every single thing in our lives, good, bad and ugly. We can start by being grateful for what is the most obvious to us, and see how our perception towards life changes. Gratitude opens the heart, and it opens the portal for rapid healing and nurturing manifestations. The magic of life will flow towards us, and every cell in our body will align with the vibration.

Once we work on showing more gratitude, the side effects can be:

We want to give more.
We have a more positive outlook on life.
More things to be grateful for appear in our lives.
We heal faster from any physical imbalance.
It is no longer possible to be depressed and angry.

I have kept a gratitude journal by my bed for many years. This is a fantastic way to reflect on the day, and always puts me in the state of being thankful. The awareness opens the heart, and lets us be open to more of the flow of grace. Being more aware of thoughts, will let go of those not serving us. Being more grateful every day, will change our lives for the better.

"Thank you, thank you, thank you!"

The two simple words that will change our lives. The energy that will invite in the love and joy that is our natural state of being. I am, through simplifying my life in every way, letting those words lead the way. You have heard me say that nature is perfect on numerous occasions. It is perfect in the sense that everything has a purpose, a place and a part in the dance of life. It is the never ending flow of life which holds all potentials. Me, I am simply a humble human, understanding that in reality I know nothing, and that the more I discover, the smaller, yet grander, I see that I am. We are all part of this magical creation, and by recognizing that, we are recognizing our home.

Nature will do this to us, awaken our true feelings and grace. I am also a very enthusiastic tree hugger, and have found that trees are not only great huggers, they are wise and very healing. Yes, they emanate this beautiful energy, this vibration, that is healing and grounding to the human body. Different trees have different frequencies, and in ancient cultures, tree hugging was a common healing practice. To be in sync with nature was natural and sacred. Everything vibrates, everything is literally vibration. Different vibrations affect biological behavior. That means that when one touches a tree, or is in the general vicinity of a tree, its different vibrational pattern will affect various biological behaviors within our body. I am following an old tradition that has been observed all around the world. Maybe the day will come when doctors will prescribe a day in the forest to those in need of healing.

In Japan, people practice forest bathing, *where they spend quiet time absorbing the wisdom of ancient forests, taking long walks among the trees to stimulate their immune system. In Taoism, students are encouraged to meditate among trees, and it is believed that the trees will absorb the negative energies, replacing them with healthy ones. Trees are seen as a source of emotional and physical healing, and as meditators, absorbing universal energies.*

In chi-quong, the teachings tell us how to align the body with the "aura" of a tree. Trees are natural processors that can help us transform our body's sick or negative energy into positive, vital life-force energy. As we connect our energy with the tree, we facilitate our own physical and emotional healing. The Taoist theory is that because trees stand very still, they are better at absorbing the energy from the earth, and the energy from the Heavens. Trees and all plants have the ability to absorb the light frequencies and transform them into physical food, and it is told they do the same with energetic food. Science is now presenting several studies on health benefits from hugging trees, but really all you have to do is to try it. Go outside, and find a tree that looks inviting. Ask it kindly if you can hug it, then embrace it and breathe deeply. I take my shoes off for some extra grounding. There is nothing like a great hug!

I have a tree friend which I call the wisdom tree, and any time I need to make a decision, or am pondering something, I ask for clarification from my friend. I go to it, take off my shoes, hug it and empty my mind. Then, I let it all go. Most often I get a very clear picture of what I need to do, or what the answer is, and sometimes it will show itself to me in due time.

Being grounded means being connected to Mother Earth. When you are physically connected, several things happen. For one, all the positive ions that are created from being surrounded by wireless, electromagnetic fields, electrical noise and sound, are balanced by the negative ions that the Earth emanates. *That* is how perfect nature is. The Earth is a natural source of electrons and subtle electrical fields. They are essential for the proper functioning of circulation, synchronization of biorhythms and other physiological processes in the human body.

Our bodies are meant to come into contact with the Earth on a regular basis. Again, the positive electrons in the form of free radicals can build up in our bodies, and direct contact with earth balances this out with its negative grounding charge. So many are suffering from being around electromagnetic waves, Wi-Fi and mobile phone waves, and many of us have a high amount of positive electrons built up in our bodies. Take a walk on the *wild* side, and take an electrical load off.

Throughout history, humans have spent time outdoors and connected with the soil. Today we are separated through shoes and high-rises. From walking on the ground barefoot, to gardening and digging in the soil, humans have always touched the earth. Now, · the Western World has moved away from nature in so many ways. We live in houses, wear rubber shoes, are exposed to EMPF's, eat chemicals and genetically modified foods, and drink un-pure water.

We have lost our contact with that which we are a part of, and are suffering the consequences.

Have you noticed how a beach vacation is soothing you, and giving you more energy? There is nothing like a long swim in the ocean, or a hike in the woods. The sand and ocean water are both naturally conductive materials. Perfect for grounding the body, removing excess positive electrons. I know, we all need some extra "vitamin sea"!

We know that hugging a tree, and walking barefoot is grounding. I have found something else that will also connect me to Mother Earth and all of her wisdom, and that is the wild herbs. Thanks to Dr.

Robert Morse, I have developed a deep passion for them. Through his teachings, I was shown the magic of the herbal kingdom. Yes, I was introduced to a world of pure magic. The wild greens, the medicinal herbs, the flowers - they are all there for us to explore and to use. I have seen profound effects on all my bodies from taking the herbal blends, and also from using them fresh from the forest. During the season, I pick the herbs fresh every single day, and blend them up in my smoothie. Some of the most potential all-round healing herbs are willingly growing right in our back yard. Many of them, we categorize as weed. Not only have we forgotten how to use them, how to appreciate the gift that they are, we also look at them as a nuisance, as weeds. The most common ones are dandelions, plantain, ground elder and stinging nettles. I am sure that most of you know about some of them, if not all of them. I pick them, rinse them, and eat them fresh, yes, even the stinging nettle. I also use birch leaves, clover, fire weed, chickweed and thistle.

I have a way of making sure that I get that magic into my body all year round, so I pick more than I need all summer, then I dry the herbs, powder them, and use them during winter. I gift the powder to others, and I am empowered by this free, easily available powerful food and medicine being there for us all. I am in awe that I am able to grow into more freedom through nature. I know, you already know this, nature really *is* perfect!

The more I consume of the wild edibles, the more connected and aware I feel. I am a firm believer that what will feed us and nurture us with the highest potential energy and nutrition is the wild edibles. The berries, the herbs, the greens, flowers and leaves. The roots and the sap, all magical and healing. Ever since I started this journey, I have gotten more and more connected with all of these plants. Through eating them, having dreams and visions, and through being around their energy - I have fund true love for nature and all the life in it. The purity and the vibration is nurturing for every cell in our body. The herbs are intelligent and tissue specific, they are true healers. What started out as a quest for healing, *physical* healing, has ended up as a passion and a calling.

The true level of healing, is the level of awareness gained.

I mentioned sap, and that is my latest experience. For 30 days, I was able to drink around 1 liter of pure fresh birch sap this last season. Wow, that is an energy-drink you will never forget having. The taste is like pure water with just a hint of sweetness. Clear and cool, straight from the tree. This is a natural ready-to-drink liquid. I was gifted this elixir from a series of birch trees that are growing in my neck of the woods. I was amazed at how easy it was to tap the tree, and how invigorating the sap was to drink. The traditional virtues of birch and its efficient removal of toxic substances from the liver and kidneys, has been known and appreciated for ages. There are very few single substances that are capable of targeting the body's two major cleansing and purification systems at the same time. It is a fantastic detoxifying elixir!

Birch trees contain powerful diuretic properties that aids in flushing out harmful toxins, uric acid, and excess water from the body. Again, it helps in maintaining good kidney and liver health, which is a welcoming trait for all of us. There are a numerous more benefits, one being its high nutritional value, another the living energy of this water. The unbeatable pure vibrating energy. *That* is what we want to ingest, the pure life-force of nature.

If you want to try this for yourself, remember to ask the tree's permission. Never tap the same tree for more than 24 hours, and always tap when the sap is rising. After that, it needs it for its own leaves. Then, remember to plug the whole that you made to ensure that the tree will not be bleeding. A grand thank you will then be in order. We are welcome to harvest the gifts of nature, but we must always show our gratitude and tread lightly.

Living in Norway, on the coast of the North Sea, has a few great benefits. While the tropics have their ripe juicy fruits, we have the wild herbs and the kelp. The kelp that I am harvesting is nothing like what I have been purchasing in any capsule or powder. This is fresh from the ocean, all pure living sea goodness. My love for the wild edibles includes the seaweed, the sea vegetables, and here, we have them in abundance, just outside my back door. Kelp is a fantastic source of nutrition, and is very high in iodine. This important mineral is a thyroid fuel, and a mineral generally lacking in a modern diet. I am not at all for counting levels of substances that we can analyze and categorize though. I believe the body will balance and take what it needs at all times, when we feed it what it needs, and not as much what it does not.

The kelp has a salty taste, and can be used on salads and in dressings, eaten as it is, raw, or dried and grounded into a powder. I have had periods when I have craved it big time, and I know that the kelp, the pure fresh ocean gold has helped my body in many ways. It is because of the kelp's support of the pituitary gland and the thyroid, that makes it the superhero of supplements for nail and hair health. My husband has been the boss of the kelp harvesting, the drying and the powdering. Me, I have been the boss of eating it. Well, I have also been the boss of staying on top of the tide table. To be able to catch the fresh kelp, still growing from their roots, calm seas and a low tide has been a must. If you are ever able to harvest your own kelp, go get it!

Now, moving onto something that will draw you in just by the smell of them. Not like kelp, these most wonderful substances are pleasure from one end to the other. Kelp might have the most fantastic properties, but once you have dried it in your house, the smell will not be what sells this plant. The essential oils on the other hand will draw you in in an instant. The essences, the anointing, healing and therapeutic essential oils, are pure joy for the sense of smell. My cup is full, only thinking about them. It is natural for us to be drawn to loving aroma. We all love a good smell, and did you know that if you smell it you eat it? Every particle that we breathe becomes a part of our physical being. Either we drink it, eat it, put it on our skin or smell it, we are ingesting it.

I had a vision some years back of me being visited by a master, and given a chamomile flower. I was told that it would show me healing and truth. I then ran across an article on chamomile essential oil, and I was sold. I went on to reading my first books on the topic, and I fell in love with the energy and the ancient history about these essential oils. The ancient Egyptians used many essential oils as medicine, and their recipes are recorded in the hieroglyphics. There are 188 references to the use of essential oils in the Bible. I am now using them on my skin, diffusing them into the air, using them in my home-made skin care products, my mouth water, my toothpaste and as my perfume. Everywhere I go people ask me what I am wearing. "You smell so good, what is it that you are wearing"? Well, just a little bit of nature here, and a little bit there. A clean fruity diet, a functioning lymphatic system, and the smell of the healing essences. No, I do not say that, I simply say, "I use the oils, no perfume, no toxic commercial perfume". My second book has amazing recipes and information regarding these oils. Make sure you look into it.

Dr. Royal Rifle's study of frequencies raises an important question concerning the frequencies of substances we eat, breathe, and absorb. Many pollutants lower healthy frequency. The frequency topic again. Listen to this: Processed food has a frequency of zero. Fresh produce has up to 15 Hz, dried herbs from 12 to 22 Hz, and fresh herbs from 20 to 27 Hz. Essential oils start at 52 Hz and go as high as 320 Hz, which is the frequency of rose oil! Wow, right? I have read that clinical research show therapeutic grade essential oils to have the highest frequency of any natural substance known to man, creating an environment in which disease, bacteria, virus, fungus, etc., cannot live. The environment, the inner terrain, it is all about creating a house where health will thrive.

I know, I have been exploring and experimenting with a myriad of different protocols, supplements and healing techniques. For years, I was like a sponge, soaking up every piece of information on healing and rejuvenation I could get my hands and eyes on. It was not that I never stopped searching, it was more that I am a curious soul by nature. I am a seeker by passion, and I love to learn and explore. I simply love to explore new things, and to look at new ideas. Like my self-talk had simplified, my natural eagerness to find out more, to seek and learn, changed dramatically. I was simplifying my intake so to speak. I found myself reading less, and listening more. Reading all those books, the education on nutrition and regeneration, had taught me to step back and look at everything from a different perspective. Everything that I had tried and re-tried, as a part of my foundation, was of great value, but the truth found me from a different place. It found me through my intuition and inner knowing.

Health and healing is simple, it is natural and effortless, change is not. Even though change is constant, the mind will resist it.

Our mind has a tendency to want to understand, to analyze and to find sense in everything. Being so capable of thinking non-stop, and feeling a little proud when solving a puzzle, anything simple is not what we are usually striving for. If things were simple, everyone would be doing them, right? Simple is boring anyway, and not challenging for our minds. We are builders, collectors and academics, we do not follow the sign of simple, it does not resemble challenge. I could ramble on, but you get my point.

A wise man once said; *"The only thing standing in the way of our wisdom is our education"*.

I kept seeing, that the more I thought I knew, the less I knew, meaning the more I thought I knew, the more I found that I did not know. At the same time, everything was getting so crystal clear to me, in a simple way. Not everything was for me to understand, it was there to be lived and observed.

Simplifying means getting rid of the obstructions and what is holding us back. The mind is a tricky thing. It will lock us into the need of understanding mentally, while the answer might be right under our noses, so to speak. The answer is most often not a mental resolution, but a simple message from our bodies. A simple direction from our own wisdom and inner knowing. Nature is a collective awareness, and effortlessly changes with every season. We, as humans, seem to have stepped out of the simplicity that is within nature. We have complicated everything from what we should eat, to how we should spend our time. We are gathering stuff, expensive cars, building enormous houses, while feeling sick, tired and lost in our own creation. Adding on, and adding on, is never the solution. We see fixing as adding, like more is always better. Let us throw in more supplements, more vitamins, more food, more toys, more achievements and more things. It all accumulates in more stress, more weight and more clutter. Less is more, and simple is freedom.

The body is such a complex organism, designed to take care of absolutely every process of functioning, all by itself. At the same time, it is amazingly easy to manage. All it needs is love, some simple foods, water, sunshine, movement and sleep. That is all! It just needs to be able to do what is designed to do! By getting out of the mind, we will be able to *know* what we need. By getting clean from poisons, acids and waste, we will be able to *hear* the clear message. I know, it sounds easy, and it *is!*

In nature, there is no obstruction, constipation, or bad choices. We can state that every choice is the right one, and that every emotion is an illusion. We can state that no matter what we live

204

or do, it is ok, and that every journey is the right one. Yet, cause and effect is still present, and by choosing a path, we will have to wear the robe, to walk our talk. Cause and effect. We are seeing the effect of not following the laws of nature, and we are paying the bill. Through sickness and stress, the lack of feeling loved and safe, we are experiencing the panic of not having or being enough. We are always enough, always. Our basic needs are simple, and few in numbers. There is no solution in complication, and there is no large puzzle to solve. There is only life, the simple exercise of breathing, loving and being. We can complicate it if we want, with but`s and reasons for hanging on to stuff, but it will not set us free. True freedom is seeing the simple in everything, and knowing that it is perfect the way it is. Nature is effortless in its growth and manifestations. We are not meant to struggle.

Just because something is simple, does not mean it is necessarily easy. It does not have to be easy. Easy to me is overrated. It was never about easy, it was about getting out of what was holding me down and sick. We all have a job to do, to bring *us* back to balance, back to nature, so to speak. The road is clear and open, all we have to do is take the first step, and to keep on walking. The road was always there, nothing is new under the sun. Nothing can ever be created that was not already there, in potential. Think about that, it is all there, and all we have to do is to love ourselves enough to start walking. I promise you, that when you start to feel what feeling good really feels like, you will never want to go back, ever.

We can never change something by doing the same thing we did to create it.

We are led to believe that we should use sunscreen to protect ourselves from the sun. The life-force, giving, nurturing sun. We are led to believe that we actually need to put chemicals on our skin. That we need to put products easily absorbed into the bloodstream on our skin. All this, to be able to be outside in the sunshine! *Hello!* *No*, the Creator/the Universe/nature did not make a mistake!

Yes, we are supposed to be in the sunshine, as it *is* giving us highly beneficial nurturing and energy on so many levels. We really need to wake up from this craziness. We are killing ourselves slowly, creating disease and suffering. Stop all sunscreen uses, and at least stop spraying it around. Use organic cold pressed coconut oil on your skin. If you wear it, you eat it. If you smell it, you eat it. If you eat it, you live and feel it. Oh yes!

If you have a fair skin tone, be in the sun less and build up. I have not worn sunscreen in years, and I am most certainly fair skinned. I used to get sun rashes, and guess what, not anymore! This is important information, this is waking up, can you feel it?

I stopped wearing sunscreen many years ago, and my skin never burns. That is not because I do not have fair skin, believe me I do. I used to have sun rashes every summer growing up. I burned very easily, but as I cleaned myself out, and healed, my skin healed too. All that congested lymph that was hiding under my skin, found its way out. I was no longer the toxic red nosed puppy while in the sun. That being said, burning is never a good idea, and until you can tolerate the sun, spend more time in the shade, or wear some light clothing. Go natural, grow FREE!

It is time to see beyond anything ever taught, and connect with source itself.

NOTE: In the book "Know the Truth and get Healthy" you will find more on how to tap a birch, harvest and dry your own kelp, and how to make your own sunscreen.

Chapter 20

Health simplified.

Our health is not a mystery, quite the opposite. It has been complicated through a whole industry. It has been complicated through science and the intellect, and it has been lost to greed and power. For me, the more I trusted nature, the simpler it got. The less I did, the more aligned with health I got. Let me share with you the simplest way I know of looking at the physical body and its health.

The body consists of two major fluids and a trillion cells. Yes, I know it is simplified, but this is the most important thing to know. We have two major fluids, blood and lymph. We are used to being very concerned with monitoring the blood. We do blood tests, and rely on what they can tell us. We are looking to our blood for irregularities to tell us how to regain health. The blood is like the kitchen in the body. It is the supplier of nutrients to all the cells. So, you can imagine how important it is to have clean blood. We need a clean kitchen. The blood also needs to stay alkaline, it needs to stay at a perfect pH of 7.34. When that changes, we lose. To keep us up and running, alive and well, the body will do anything in its power to make sure the blood stays balanced. When too many acids are present, it will make sure the blood stays within its pH. It will do so by drawing alkaline minerals from the bone and tissue. The blood needs to stay in balance, and the rest of the body will have to suffer. When acids happen, we feel pain.

The body is a perfectly designed self-healing mechanism. It is self-cleansing, and therefor has a sewer system, the lymphatic system. Every cell in the human body needs to eat and poop. Yes, like you and me, they are no different. The waste is carried from the cells via the lymphatic system, to the eliminative organs. The shit needs to come out, there is no other way. If the acids stay in, we are in pain, and if acids win, we lose. This is what I have experienced firsthand. All so called disease, comes from not eliminating waste. Stagnant lymph, acids, toxins, all directly linked to less than optimal health. Acidosis comes from acid forming food, anger, fear and stress. There are thousands of small septic tanks called lymph nodes throughout the body. They are little holding tanks, or septic tanks, that are used by the lymph system to filter and destroy pathogens, toxins, antigens, etc.

Digestion, absorption, utilization, and elimination.

First, we need to digest the food that we are eating to be able to absorb the nutrients. A good digestion needs enzymes and the proper digestive acids, and we know that digestion starts in the mouth. We then absorb, it is through the villi of the small and large intestines. Utilization is where the blood comes in, and involving the liver and glands, for hormones, the blood carries the nutrition to every cell. Now, we are getting to the elimination. Most of what we put in, must come out. This is where we are clogged up and easily get congested and overly acidic. The main eliminative organs are the skin, the lungs, the kidneys and the colon.

The simplicity that I learned from Dr. Robert Morse, blew me away; "The body is like a city", he says. "The immune and lymphatic systems act like a police force and a sanitation department. It picks up the trash from each house/cell in the city, depending on the lifestyle within each house, the type of waste and the amount of it, will vary. The lymph system, along with its immune cells, has the job of protecting and keeping the body clean. Many foods that people routinely eat clog up this system, and then what happens? The waste is not being picked up, and it becomes smelly, burning, gassy and painful to be around. So, there you go, we need to take the waste from the house to the dumping ground. We need to clean the septic tanks, and we need every part of the process to flow on a daily basis."

The kidneys are filtering out lymphatic waste, and sadly, for most of us, our kidneys are not able to do that job. When the kidneys suffer, we suffer. I tell people to pee in a jar. If you are seeing urine clear as day, and no sediments floating around, you are not filtering.

The adrenals are a major key to our health, as they sit on top of the kidneys, which again, filter out lymphatic waste. This is crucial to a healthy body. We know the lymphatic system is the sewer system of the body, and if we do not get the cellular and the metabolic waste out, we will burn from the acids. This is called disease, or an acidic body.

Any kind of stress, emotional or physical, will put a strain on the adrenal glands. When eating meat, we are consuming the animals' stored adrenalin, which will of course stress our adrenals. We have all heard of adrenal fatigue, but did you know that anxiety is a sign of burnt adrenals also? Adrenal and kidney "failure" is the root cause of most diseases, as they are the key to carrying out the lymphatic waste. We are made of over a trillion cells, and two major fluids. Blood and lymph. The blood feeds, the lymph cleans. Feeding the cells will not create optimal health, without cleaning out the sewage.

The glands are the government, and they control most everything. This is why gland health is so important, and why so many of our symptoms arise from weakened glands. What will weaken a gland? Acids again, mucus, stagnant lymph around the gland. Any weak organ or gland most often also has a weak state from birth, but we know about regeneration. The body will regenerate when it is given a chance.

The answer to any health concern is always alkalization, detoxification and regeneration!

Leave the animal proteins, eat mostly fruits, melons and berries, and know that the body is an amazing self-healing organism. Detoxification is an art, and a way of letting the body get rid of the waste that is burning and damaging the cells.

What we do not eliminate we accumulate.

We have a species specific diet, like every other creature on this planet. We are primates. What we are witnessing is what happens when we really, I mean *really* move away from that, and feed our bodies dead, altered chemistry. All animals that are taken off their diets get sick. Animals in the care of humans often get diseases. Wild animals don't get those, how could they? Something to think about? What we are eating is killing us. Period! When we look around, and start counting those over 50 not taking pills, having a happy, positive, strong, athletic, healthy, glowing, natural body - they are few and far between. We could even start counting those over 30, and have a hard time finding someone with no glasses, no digestive issues, skin issues, weight issues or emotional imbalances.

Children are now being diagnosed with what used to be old people's "diseases". That should get the big red light to go off for all of us. Their weakened handed down glands and organs, together with a poor diet, contributes to ill health and depression.

Un-clean water, lack of movement, sunshine, lack of sleep and rest, all factors that rob the body of health. The thing is, that what we put in our mouth, what we feed our cells, what vibration we choose to reside in, will lead us to the rest of our choices. Every generation is getting weaker. We are the ones passing those weak genes on to our children, let us take responsibility by healing our bodies, and strengthening our organs and glands. Through detoxification, alkalization, hydration and regeneration, we can restore what nature has so perfectly created.

Honor God and creation, by honoring yourself.

The longer I stay raw, the healthier I get, and the more passionate I am becoming. Not just about life and health, but also about sharing this message. I see so much suffering, and I am sure that you do too. Being healthy is rare, and even those not being healthy feel they are, as it is the new norm to not be free of imbalances. We are adopting to feeling less than optimal, and that scares me. I also remember what pain and suffering feels like, and how eating what I am designed to eat has been a large part in changing my life and health. We need to love ourselves more. Really love ourselves. Once you really love yourself, you cannot hurt yourself any longer, or anyone else for that matter. Power up and take charge for the children, as they are looking to us for guidance and direction.

We can all start by changing what we are putting in our mouth. There is no mystery diet, supplement or ritual you need to do. Health is not something that we do not know how to achieve. It is as simple as the raw living high-vibrating foods that nature has provided for us. Simple and perfect.

Let me tell you about the fruits, the great detoxifiers. They are perfect for us, just as they are. They are hydrating and regenerating, and every cell thrives on the simple sugars. Forget about fruits having too much sugars. Not at all. Simple sugar is what every cell needs, so stop starving them. Fruits are alkaline forming, together with vegetables, some nuts and seeds. By eating fruits, we are eating what the body was designed to digest, and nothing will clog up the sewer system. It is important to be aware that fruits digests very rapidly. They do not sit in the stomach for long, or in the intestines. When you eat anything else, before fruits, like fats, protein, and starches, the fruits will be sitting, waiting to get moving, and start to ferment in the process. This is called bad food combining and will lead to indigestion and a lot of fun for our uninvited guests. Be aware that even vegetables digest slower than fruits, so eat fruits alone. Cooking any food will alter its chemistry, create acids and destroy its enzymes.

My deepest cleansing so far, happened on my 62-day grape fast. I embarked on a journey of eating grapes only, for the period of 62 days. Grapes are fantastic healers, and they are astringent lymphatic movers. At the same time, they stimulate the kidneys to filter out the waste. For me, they were showing me how deep cleaning can be experienced. After 30 days, I hit a really high fever, showing me that my body was cleaning out some deep seated toxins. My kidneys were filtering like crazy, showing clouds and particles in my urine. My bladder felt like I was burning up with acids, and I was. My symptoms resembled a urinary tract infection, and lasted for about 6 days. Quite a strong cleansing experience.

Eat the color, the juiciness, the fiber, the nutrition, the vibration, the hydration and the healing power of plain God given fruits!

Be on the winning team, and fuel your body
with food designed for man.
Be gentle with yourself, and say yes to the juices of life.
Be aware, and make better choices for your family.
Know that real food is health promoting.
Know that your health is in your hands.

Know that you always have a choice to be the best that you can be.
Feel the joy of eating organic, clean, living foods.
Feel the compassion from embracing nature.
Feel inspired from letting go of what is not serving you.
Fruits are packed with vitamins, micronutrients and minerals.
Fruits are hydrating to every cell.
Fruits are filled with fiber.
Fruits have the life-force of nature itself.
Fruits are loaded with antioxidants.
Fruits are high in simple sugars which feed every cell in the body.
Fruits are alkalizing to the body.
Fruits support regeneration of cells.
Live in compassion for men and animals.
Live free of disease and suffering.
Live lightly on this earth and choose to be happy.

Chapter 21

The choice.

This is my favorite topic, self-empowering. This is what I breathe and live for, to inspire. My mission and my passion has melted together into one thing, making sure that anyone who crosses my path knows how powerful they are. Powerful beyond words. Get ready to handle it, because you are *it!*

I am on the crystal bed at the salt cave, Naples Florida. I have been here before, and I am always eager to spend time in this amazing place. As I lie on the bed, I have seven crystals hanging over me. They are pointing towards my chakras. They are extremely clear and highly polished Vogel cut quartz crystals, suspended approximately 12 inches above me. Each of the quartz crystals have been cut to a specific frequency. Colored lights, chosen to match the frequency of chakra colors, radiate light and energy through the crystals to each respective chakra. They shine on and off in certain rhythms to cleanse, balance, and align our energies. I am bathing in the energy, clearing my mind, giving thanks. I drift off, and am awakened by the intense burning in my hands. Both my hands are burning hot, and a clear voice says, "The healing is in your hands!" It was loud and clear, and I got the message. It is all us, it always was and always will be.

Saying that health is a choice, is a bold statement that often draws out a lot of but`s. I know, it is bold. The only thing that drove me out of bed, against all odds, and against all so called reason, was that one thing, I *chose* to do so. I made a choice, and I stuck with it. I started walking, and I did not stop, no matter what. I never will. To me, having a choice simply means that we have the free will to take responsibility for any health, or life issue, and that through determination and education, we can walk from where we are to where we want to be. Life is what we all want out of life. We want to live more than anything else, and yet, living seems to be the hardest part. Living is so much more than breathing, and only when we fall out of health, do we tend to see the value of living in an amazing healthy body. When the body is functioning, life is always more fun.

Even though it might not always feel that way, you hold the power to change where you are going. It's ok to not feel happy and inspired all the time. The most important thing is to not make that your story. The story you tell about your life is the story you keep living.

Your story is the things that you tell yourself and others every day. Sometimes it is even an old story, so old it might not even be as true as you remember it to be. Holding on to old stories can be comforting, even though they might be hurtful. The words you use are your crayons, and every day you are given a blank piece of paper to draw and write on.

"Don't look back unless you are going that way".

Often what is holding us back from achieving our goals, is the way we define ourselves through our past experiences. Sometimes there is forgiveness that has to be granted, to let go of the old, and sometimes there are patterns that need to be addressed. Whatever it is that keeps you chained to a story that is not aligned with the future you would like, it is time to let it go. When we speak to and about others, we are blessing or cursing, and the same thing goes for speaking about and to ourselves. Being aware of this, can help us to reshape our reality. With some work and dedication, it is possible to rewrite the story that does not serve the future.

Letting go of the story is like setting free what has been holding us back.

Again, we are all the same. From the core, all humans seek to be happy and healthy. We all want a good life, whatever that means to us. To me, I found that having a body that was in a huge amount of pain, not giving me a chance to do any of the things that I loved, was a deal breaker. It was not the life that I wanted. I had to rewrite my story, and change what I was doing. If you want something to change, change something.

We have the power to change our lives, yet most often we do not want to own that power. It seems we would rather stay miserable than to change. We find some sort of comfort in the known, and we hold on to it, even though it is hurting us. Every day, every moment, holds a choice. We can choose to be happy, free, loving, a good friend, helpful, and to take care of our bodies. We can choose to smile, laugh and have a positive outlook on life. We can choose to see the best in all, and to do no harm. The list is endless, as life is a fluent manifestation of your constant choices. It can be hard to take responsibility for our own lives, yet more and more people are doing it.

So, if all it takes is to change what we are doing, to step up and take charge, then why is it so hard? Well, we fear the unknown, and fear is a cold breeze we do not like to feel. We tend to be controlled by the fear of life itself. The underlying fear of death, illness, failure and loss, becomes larger than the pure joy of living. Our natural state is to be eager and enthusiastic about every moment of life, and to be able to change and grow without fear.

Once you become fearless life becomes limitless.

So much of what we are experiencing is brought on by fear. The deep rooted fear, that distorts everything. When we are in pain, for example, it is most often not the pain itself that is intolerable, but what it represents. The fear of not knowing if and when it will pass. The uncertainty of why it is there. Is something wrong with me? Am I in danger? This is what turns fear into suffering. Pain is just pain, but fear is suffering. If someone could tell you that you would be 100% fine, and the exact time the pain would pass, most likely you would deal with the pain very differently. This is what gets interesting when working towards being more fearless. The fear of the unknown fades, and freedom arises. Freedom gives a sense of calm and enthusiasm, that keeps us strong and motivated during trying and challenging times. We all have them, the trying times, they are called life. It is what we do with them that makes the difference. So called challenges can be used as stepping stones, motivators and most of all teachers. If we see them as obstacles, deal breakers or failures, that is what we will get.

It is our natural instinct to be fearless, invincible, unstoppable and strong. We are all amazingly *powerful*! Our energy can transmute anything, and no ill health can live within joy, truth, calmness and faith. Fear and doubt will tear us apart, so we need to go deep, meditate and really get to the core of who we are. There, we are powerful beyond this body.

We must let go of our fear of death, as it is only a transformation, and let this life be a journey of eagerness and bold actions. There is never anything to lose, but one's own perception of this life. This is the most powerful underlying cause of all lack of change. Fear of death. I read many years ago that before we embrace death, we are not truly living. Oh boy, did I experience that to be true.

When I let go of clinging to what *was*, clinging to what I thought I wanted and needed, a huge shift happened. I was no longer holding on, and allowed change to happen. To be able to receive what is best for *you*, you must be willing to let go of everything you think you need.

I was ready to give it all up, it did not matter, I was ready to let go of *everything*.

These are the choices that we all have, including you my friend. The magic in your life is yours to create, every day, in every moment. The power of change is blowing, and what that means to you, and your life, is *your* decision to make.

Change is continuous, it is the nature of the Universe. Progress is a choice, a commitment to self. The power of *you* is where the magic is. I remember so well chasing time, running from appointment to appointment, never feeling content. I also remember the self-medicating with caffeine, cigarettes, alcohol and food. We use these substances to run from our feelings, our lives and our emotions. I got my health and life back, and you can do the same. Take charge, and take your health and joy to the next level!

Say yes to organic natural plant foods, vaccine-free lives, fairness, love, happiness, prosperity, inner peace and kindness.

Say no to animal cruelty, and let compassion be our game. More and more people are standing up for what they believe in, educating themselves, seeing their own power and grace, and feeling the anticipation of positive change.

Again, if you want something to change, change something, and remember, change is what will get you to where you want to go.

Change is blowing, and we can all feel the wind.

Feel your own strength and your ability to choose life! Say *yes* to all that serves you, and fear nothing. *Be* the change you want to see in this world, and know that *you* are the one you have been waiting for. Life here on earth is too short not to love, laugh, play and dance fearlessly. Step up to your full potential, and take charge of your destiny. Every cell in your body is at your command, and every thought, emotion and food you eat, is serving you in one way or another. You always get what you ask for, even though you might not even know that you asked.

You are so much stronger than you might think.

You hold the power within to change your entire life, not just your health, but everything. You *are* the change, and only your own doubts, fears and thought patterns can set you back from your goals. Like the dandelion, growing through the asphalt, you can do what your mind might see as impossible. It is growing through something that we see as so much stronger than the plant. We are seeing the impossible in action. Not everything can be comprehended by the mind, and not every solution is within our perception. Always keep your focus on your goal, on the solution, and do not get mental about the how and the when. Sometimes the how is way beyond our comprehension, and the creation is so much larger than our thoughts. The strength we all hold, the power within, and the ability to choose, is true freedom.

Freedom is knowing you have what it takes. Knowing is only of value when put into action. Action is the driving force of any manifestation. The next time you see a dandelion, remember how strong you are!

219

There is no rejection, only redirection.

What if there is no rejection? The thought keeps me in a flow, and looking back, boy did I keep banging on those closed doors! Often we tend to think ahead of ourselves, meaning we imagine events or situations, and we feel a sense of being let down or rejected if things do not work out. We have made a manual of how things should work, and when things do not take that direction, we see failure or lack of success. When one door closes, another one opens. Right? True story. When a door is closed, we are given the opportunity to move on, it is simply the Universe's way of telling us that this is not serving our highest good. There is no rejection, only Gods protection.

By faith, the redirection can flow, and by giving thanks for new opportunities, they will become many. Faith is such a key word to moving easier through life. Without faith, how can one leap on to new and unfamiliar ground? Sometimes we get a door slammed in our face, and are redirected in a way that feels overwhelming. I know, this has happened to me many times. You get the feeling that wow, why is this not working? That is the time you want to step back and pause. Let that door be, accept it, and walk on. I am sure you have experienced what has felt as a letdown, or an event that looked bad at the moment, just to find that it turned out better than you could have imagined at the end?

Think of all the times you have looked back, thinking, oh my, if that did not happen, *this* amazing thing never would!

The word rejection means "to refuse to accept, submit to, believe, or make use of". So that simply means; the action which was rejected was not accepted at that time, and that something else will be. The timing was not optimal, and you were more needed elsewhere.

Not too long ago, my husband and I were searching for a home in Florida. We thought we had found the perfect place. We went to a number of open houses and private viewings, but nothing seemed right. We changed town, and now, we were bidding on several units, but everything seemed to fall through. I had seen this pattern before, and was aware that we were being redirected. The thing was, that I had my trip to Florida planned already, and had been searching for a place to rent for my 6 week stay. This was for February, and I had started looking early September, but nothing. What was going on? I found no condo to rent, and as we were already looking to buy, I thought, ok, maybe we will buy instead before February. Fall came and left, still nothing. We were putting in offers, but they all fell through. My flight was early February, and by mid-December I was wondering what was going on. It would be too late to buy, as the closing would take months, and still there was nothing to rent. A last resort would be to spend 6 weeks in a hotel, which was not on my wish list at all.

Two days before Christmas, we were presented this amazing unit, right in our dream neighborhood. All perfectly decorated, meeting all of our needs. We jumped right in, and closed the very same day that I landed in Florida! This is a great example showing that sometimes, things just need to get aligned, and that all those closed doors were merely redirections.

"Once the fear of rejection is set free, the door to change opens" Hilde

Again, we are back to the fear, and letting go. I love that everything is simplifying. The less we think, ponder and worry, the more life will flow towards us. By letting go of everything, we gain everything. The is the paradox that haunts us. We tend to believe that the more we hold on to what we already have, the more we will get. Quite the opposite is true. The less we hold on to, the more we will gain, on every level. Look at the body, we can use reflection; The more we hold on to, being old emotional baggage, foods or toxins, the more toxic, heavy and constipated we get. The body tends to hold on to more physical weight when we hold on to emotional baggage. A thriving, light, healthy and balanced body, has no excess of anything. There is no need to not walk lightly and free. Life is about the simple glow of energy, inviting us in as an open door.

When you love life, life loves you back. What you give your attention to, grows. What you resist, persists. What you send out, comes back to you.

Chapter 22

Being authentic.

Being true to *you*, is being true to Creation, and being authentic means being true to *you*. Any walk towards a life of freedom will require authenticity. It is the effect of stepping up to full responsibility. For me, it has been a gradual process, and maybe the toughest one. Fist I had to realize that I was not being, or living an authentic life. Then, I had to be willing to look that in the eye, and say goodbye to the impression of me that I had been clinging to. As my body was healing, and I did not longer need my masks and my shields, I gradually became more true to *me*, more authentic in every way.

As I am walking, barefoot in the rain, inhaling the smell of fall, I think, what is all this bullshit? I mean, what is all this not being authentic and true to oneself at all times?

I am pondering this my whole walk, feeling into what it is about these times that seems to push so many to the edge, so to speak. There is so much anger, despair, illness, frustration, not feeling content, and longing for something more, something out there, longing for change. The longing is a bell ringing, saying, "listen, let me be *me*! Let me be myself, let it be safe to be *me*!"

It is almost like everything is being shattered, driven to the surface, like every old trauma, hurt and emotional upheaval is showing up at the front door, saying: "Here I am, now deal with me"!

I keep thinking about my life, about how everything has changed from the core over these last 8 years. There has been a massive transformation in my health, a transformation and a shift in consciousness for sure, a spiritual awakening, oh yes indeed! Still, looking back, one of the things I have noticed the most, is that I dare to live more authentically. At least I am striving to, every day. To be living my own truth, showing up as me, and trusting that I'll always be enough, is what I believe has changed my life the most. It has been such great part of my healing. Being bullshit-free is true freedom!

Through our social conditioning and programming, we have all been led from our truth. From our upbringing, and from fear based information, we have all been mended and formed. We are most often pleasers and what I call "bullshitters". Our lives get to be an altered version of our truth and purpose, and now we are wondering why we feel lost and in ill- health.

I see so many that struggle with their health on both the physical and the emotional level, from not living authentically. Wearing any mask, is an obstruction of life. Every minute that we are not living our truth, we are in fact hurting ourselves. Have you noticed how it feels when you are pleasing others, just to keep the peace? Have you noticed that your body is feeling heavy after you have been acting fine, when you are not? This is all taking a toll on the physical body. Not expressing truth is acidic to every cell, and it is suffocating to the soul. It is also keeping us from living the life we truly deserve.

- *Being authentic, simply means to live your truth, and to walk your talk.*

- *It means to stand up for what you believe in, and to know your real power.*

- *It means to not let fear rule your actions or your feelings.*

- *It means knowing that it is ok to fully express yourself.*

- *It means that you can live from your place of true passion.*

From my own experience, I can see that knowing what your truth is, can be hard. For so many years, I believed I was living my truth, but in fact I was not being authentic at all. I was trying to be, do, and have what I believed was expected of me.

- *Truth is what comes to the surface when the obstructions are gone.*

- *Truth is what feels good to you, even though others might not feel the same way.*

- *Truth is what your soul is telling you is right for you.*

Start your authentic living by shredding some false beliefs, and by letting go of some old hurts. I am challenging you to step up and to raise your vibration, and I guarantee you will want to keep going.

If you want to live more authentically, these are great issues to take a look at:

225

Make a decision to take charge of your own life. Sometimes we tend to give the authority to someone else. Most of us have been taught to obey. It is natural to want to fit in at school, to seek acceptance at the work place. It is what we have been taught is important. I like this saying: " *What others think of you, is none of your business".*

Eat what is actually good for you. Look at what you are eating. Is it serving you? Are you supporting your body, being true to it? Eating fresh fruits and vegetables, like nature intended will raise your vibration, and start a process towards more authentic living. Being authentic is also about feeding your cells what you *know* they need, and you do, we all do.

Surround yourself with supportive people. We all need to feel that we belong. We are all in the need of support and sister/ brotherhood. Find likeminded people that will see you for who you are, and that makes being you amazing.

Speak your truth. Before speaking, I try my very best to follow this rule: *"Is it true, is it kind, is it necessary?"* Speaking one's truth, means to express what you believe in, and to stand up for yourself and others. It means to fearlessly show who you are, in every way.

Trust your intuition. Listen to your inner guidance. Only you know what is best for you, always. Trust and have faith that you are everything you need, and that it is ok to live as you desire.

Walk your talk. Live your truth, and feel confident to live your passion. Be the change you want to see!

Forgive all. It is amazing how much we can hold on to that is not serving us. Through meditation and inner searching, letting go of old hurts is a great way to find inner calm and truth. Listen to your breath, it speaks to you.

"Once we are authentic in our expressions, we will grow FREE!"- Hilde

These statements credited to Mother Teresa comes to mind, I thought they would fit nicely here, as a reminder to all of us. These words serve as a great reminder that there really is nothing outside of us, to hold us back. There is no rejection, only redirection.

If you are kind, people may accuse you of selfish, ulterior motives. Be kind anyway.

If you are successful, you will win some unfaithful friends and some genuine enemies. Succeed anyway.

If you are honest and sincere, people may deceive you. Be honest and sincere anyway.

What you spend years creating, others could destroy overnight. Create anyway.

If you find serenity and happiness, some may be jealous. Be happy anyway.

The good you do today, will often be forgotten. Do good anyway.

Give the best you have, and it will never be enough. Give your best anyway.

In the final analysis, it is between you and God. It was never between you and them anyway.

Every day might not seem like a great day to celebrate, but there is always something to be grateful for. The air that you breathe, the smell of a flower, the fresh foods on you plate, or a hug from a loved one.

Hilde Larsen

Being alive, is in itself worth celebrating, and loving yourself is the best way of showing gratitude and appreciation. It might feel strange at first, but when you think about it, what could be more amazing?

**Every breath we take, every move we make,
every thought we think, every feeling we feel,
is what we consciously choose to create.**

"I declare to live authentically, true to myself,
in gratefulness, in service, with my tribe,
to love myself, to express my truth,
and to allow myself anything that serves me.
I declare to honor my life and nature,
and to walk my talk."
Hilde

Chapter 23

Be Inspired!

To be inspired, is to acknowledge that you are alive, and that your life is a gift worth celebrating. What makes or keeps one inspired is the love for life, and the realization that the experience is completely one's own. That we can change any situation or outcome, would not be correct to state, but that we can change any perception, feeling or experienced moment, absolutely!

When life knocks at your door with a tale of ill health, you need to know that the message is simply a directional hint. When your body is talking to you, take the first hint, and know that you are a team. To be inspired and enthusiastic is a state of positive charge, and it can be aimed at any situation in life. Health is only one of them. My perspective on life has been flipped around 360 degrees, as I have gone from sleeping to being awake. I have seen how much energy I used to spend lost in the stories, the everyday hustle, appearance, achievements and chasing the good feeling. Feeling good about life is natural, and so is being happy. It is not something we need to chase after, like a drug or a fix. Being inspired is natural, and the more I dropped what was holding my energy down, the more inspired I got. The more I take off of what was never me in the first place, the clearer I get. I mean, not only clearer in my mental thinking, although that also. I mean clearer in being *me*, being able to express myself.

There is also the spirit connection that took me like a storm, once I connected to true healing on all levels. Being inspired cannot describe how amazing it feels to feel connected and safe. Knowing that you are always home, that everything is taken care of, and that this life is merely a voyage, is freeing beyond words. By decalcifying your pineal gland, the awareness will raise automatically. Fluoride in the water supply and toxins in our foods, contribute to calcifying this very important gland. All our glands are connected to our chakras, and the pineal gland is our third eye. To clear out any obstruction and find true vibrational health, we need to eat what is of that high vibration. The highest nutritional and electrical-energy foods on the planet are fresh raw fruits, vegetables, herbs, seaweeds, nuts and seeds.

Use life as your motivation, and let your future inspire you. Change takes action, and action takes motivation. Motivation takes inspiration, and inspiration comes from your inner desire to live and thrive. To find your inner desire, find stillness. From stillness, you can listen. From letting your mind rest, your true inspiration can shine through. Stop what is not serving you, and do more of what is.

Life is full of potentials, and you are the most powerful being in your life.

Focus on what matters the most.
Spend time with people who love you and that will lift your spirit.
Spend time with those who make you feel good, who make you laugh and who wants you to do better.

Focus on what you like, what you enjoy, and what makes you smile every day.
Focus on what is true to you.
Let go of anything that is holding you back, and set yourself free.
Walk lightly, and live freely.
Allow yourself to be grateful, and to receive love.
Give yourself permission to be free, to be happy and whole.
Find support and spend your time with those that lift your spirit.

Passion is an expression of the soul, a recognition of home. When we are passionate about something, about anything, everything else fades. We are in the flow, in the zone, time flies by, and we feel at peace. Passion is the train that will take us places, if we let it. It is the fuel that feeds our soul, and what makes the ride seem effortless. Do more of what you are passionate about, and watch the passion for life grow. The ride will take you to new places, make you evolve and want to serve more. Watch how everything grows, and fuels your life. Watch how everything changes, when life becomes a journey fueled by passion and purpose.

I love to tell people how amazing they are, how amazing *you* are! More often than not, people will not believe that they are. Why is this so hard for most of us to believe? We walk around completely unaware of the very fact that we are pure wonders of creation. Do you know how amazing you really are? I mean, not in a narcissistic sort of way. Not in the way that you are better than anyone else, or that you are without fault. We all have potential to be and do better. None of us are perfect, yet we all are.

You are amazing, because you are unique.
You are amazing, because you have what nobody else has.
You are amazing, because you are a manifestation of God.
You are amazing, because you have the ability to help someone else.
You are amazing because you can create.
You are amazing because you are pure love.

You are amazing because you are you!

Tell someone how amazing they are today, and start living like your true self. When looking at ourselves as amazing, or wonderful, is too hard to do, telling someone else that very thing is a great place to start.

It is time to let go of all the bullshit. It is time to let go of anything and everything that makes you believe you are not good enough. Be inspired to act as amazingly as you can. Feel how everything changes when you allow yourself to feel and act in the same direction. Know that you have what it takes. You are worthy, and you are ready.

I turned 50 this year, yet I feel inspired to create and grow, more than I ever did before. This awakening has made me reflect on the concept of aging, and how society sees age, illness and suffering, as companions. They go together. The older we get, the sicker we get. More pain, more weight, more illness, and more suffering. The body is renewable, and new cells are born every second. It is natural to be healthy at any age. Getting older does not mean getting sick, losing vision or hearing, lack of mobility or getting weaker. The body does not get sick because it has lived for a long time, but because it has been exposed to toxins and obstructions for too long. It is all about accumulation, lack of elimination.

We become what we hold on to, on all levels.

The older I get, the better I feel. Why? Because I finally understand what health is all about! It is all about showing up and taking charge, using what is there, the wisdom of the body, and the perfection of nature. What you eat is the single most important thing in your physical *and* emotional health. Logic, right there, truth and inspiration. We are highly evolved vibrational beings, made to be fueled by nature. By fuel I mean clean fresh ripe natural living foods, sunshine, fresh air and source energy.

What happens to all our bodies, the physical, the emotional and the spiritual, when we consume low energy, damaged, altered so called foods, we will know, in time. It is only a matter of time, before we see detrimental changes in the body. What are we seeing? Stiff bones, impaired vision, blood sugar issues, damaged cells, loss of hearing and mental abilities, and much more. Wait a minute, this sounds like aging! *Yes*, that is what aging really is, a buildup of waste from a lifestyle less than optimal. Adding on the weak genes handed down by generations, we see the typical aging symptoms arise even earlier. "We live longer", you might say. Not really. We live longer, sick and diseased, than some timelines, and way shorter than others. The human body is designed to be healthy, not to get sick before ending its existence here. It is natural to be heathy at any age!

Living free of guilt, letting go of old hurts and emotional stress, eating free flowing living foods, and letting the body get rid of the waste, will help the body live healthy at any age.

Fruits, along with their skin and seeds, contain valuable antioxidants that reduce the amount of free radicals in the body, as well as help to slow down the aging process. Leafy green vegetables also provide antioxidants that not only help slow down the process of aging, but also reduce many risks of age related diseases caused by a lifetime of exposure to free radicals, which are an obstruction. Herbs are here for us, the wild foods. Nature provides, if we will only listen.

Imagine me having lived so many experiences, been so many times around the sun, and still feeling like life is just beginning. I feel like I am just starting to see the real purpose and meaning of me being here. To be able to be a mother to my two amazing children is beyond words, and to be a grandmother, well, I had no idea it was even possible to feel so blessed. Through living my story, walking my talk, helping others, and seeing that life is so much more than this physical reality, I have been blessed with the opportunity to grow more FREE every day. From lying in bed for several years, too sick to get out of the house, spending years on letting this body heal, to be able to travel and play, is a journey worth living. My experience can now benefit others, and together we will walk from pain to joy, from HELL to Inspired.

I feel younger than I have felt in years, and I know this is only the beginning! How cool is that? Life just keeps getting better every single day. I am humble and grateful beyond words.

If I can do it, *you* can do it! You are powerful beyond your imagination, and your life is in your hands. Wherever you are at this very moment, is only a starting point. By loving yourself more every day, the life that you see around you will inspire you into action. My greatest wish is that by reading this book, you feel ready and enthusiastic about embarking on your own journey. It does not matter if you are labeled chronic, tired of everything, in pain, just curious about health or want to lose weight. It really does not matter. You still hold the power to take the next step, and I know that you can do it.

TO YOU WHO NEED IT!

To all of you that are going through emotional clearings right now. Know that you are not alone, and that the energies are supportive of letting it all go. Old hurts, even from your ancient family timelines will eventually surface to be cleared. The power is always within you, and you've got this. Feel the support from your whole Tribe, and know that the rest of your soul family is walking beside you. Use your true power, and *know* that you are worthy.

Say these lines out loud, and know it is so:

"I can no longer get hurt by words,
I know that they are never personal.

I will no longer raise my voice and get emotional,
I do not engage in other people's drama.

I can no longer be treated badly or unfairly,
I am removing myself from those energies.

I can no longer get disappointed,

I hold no expectations.

I do not need to shed any more tears,
my heart is now open to love and compassion.

I will no longer feel lonely,
I am never alone.

I will no longer feel unloved,
I am loved by me, in the light of the Creator.

I am free to choose to be loved and treated like the amazing,
strong, beautiful, compassionate, and courageous soul that I AM!"

Power up, and step up to the next level of your life.

You are amazing. Know it, Feel it, Act like it!

Walk with me!

AFTERWORD

My dear friends, tribe and love-family.

My wish and declaration is that you, dear reader, will continue down the path to the life that you desire and love. Through determination and faith, I see you finding what you have been searching for. You are worthy, and you are beautiful. Your life is a blessing, and we are all in this together. Life is a journey, not a destination, and I wish you an amazing travel. My walk will continue, filled with valleys and mountaintops. As long as we keep walking in eagerness and truth, the experience will be of great value, to ourselves and to those around us.

It is in gratitude that I want to share with you a short summary of one of the most creative, eventful years in my life so far. This book has been my dream for many years, and to be able to share this story with you, is a joy from my heart.

After having spent so many years in what felt like more of a dormant state, this year started off on the fast track, with me standing in front of the camera for the very first time. With wonderful help from the Zparkl Team, I made my first online video program, "Life transforming detoxification and cleansing program". It set the stage for a year of creating and playing both online and offline.

Right after finishing the video shoots, the documents and the texts, I was off to do the hand-over of our brand new Naples Florida condo. What a true blessing! This has become my new playground, my sanctuary, my healing, and my place of resetting my alignment.

My website (http://inspiredbyhilde.com/) was created all through the spring and summer, and I am very proud of how it turned out. It is created to be a place of learning and inspiration, and it is constantly evolving and changing. I had some fantastic help, and I am forever grateful for my new team and co-creators. New pages are added, and new products will be offered.

We all experience life taking a turn we do not expect, and for me this year, it was breaking my hip on April the 27th. It happened as a freak accident when I was feeling my absolute best in years. A set back? Well, yes, you might say that, but I kept learning and experiencing. I received so much love and support, observing my body healing at an amazingly rapid rate. I was confined to bed for a few months, which was letting me focus even more on my creations. I was left with metals in my body, and I'm counting on being able to have it all removed during this year.

This was also the year of my 50th time around the sun. I had such an amazing celebration. My family surprised me, making sure the day was perfect, and some beautiful women in Naples joined me for a whole day of raw food blessings.

In November I joined my soul family in Port Charlotte yet again, for the School of Detoxification. A family reunion, and fuel for my soul. What a blessed time. A time to play and learn, share and support.

I have been making several videos with Dr. Robert Morse, and I am sure there are many more to come. I have several video-series in the making, so watch out for those.

I created my first of many e-books, which was a lot of fun. The book that you have just read, has been in my heart for many years, and this was the right time for it to birth.

Looking back, I can see how the healthier we get, the clearer the mind, the more playful the soul, the more *life* we get out of life.

I have had the pleasure to meet so many new friends this year, especially in Florida. True soul friends, and for that I am forever grateful.

The feedback that I have gotten, through messages and e-mails are appreciated beyond words. The people that I see healing, the praises and the confidence in me, leaves me humble and fueled. I truly am the blessed one, for being able to do what I am so passionate about.

I have really experienced the power of the essential oils. I was blown away by the healing they promoted after my hip surgery. I knew they were potent, but I have seen some real magic, and they are now a part of my every day protocol.

I have been visiting a healing Salt Cave, and lying on John of Gods crystal bed. I have also been in a Cryotherapy full body chamber at minus 240 degrees Fahrenheit. This last year, I have had more massages than most of the previous year`s put together. I have really felt the benefits from touch, self-love and relaxation.

I have been able to join a small farming community, that lets us participate in the whole growing process. This way, I have been blessed with organic, locally grown, self-picked produce for a long season. Friends has offered home grown berries, and I have kept on picking the wild edibles. This spring, I drank fresh birch sap every day for a whole month. Highly recommended!

I have kept healing on all levels, regenerating and growing. I travelled alone to Florida for the very first time! I was told that I would never be able to live without all the terrible prescription drugs that were slowly killing me. I was told that I would have a painful future, and that I would never walk normally again. They were all so very wrong, and to understand what health is all about is the most freeing experience. I truly feel free again, and blessed to know that healing is *my* responsibility. No matter how sick, how depressed, and no matter how much you suffer, it can all change.

I love all of you, and I'm so excited to keep on walking.

"Thank you" are the words of gratitude, the words of healing. Through being grateful, we find more to be grateful for. The practice of gratitude, of forgiveness and being willing to serve, I believe to be the strongest driving forces of the love energy.

This world needs all the love that it can get, and we are all called forth to do our part.

Research shows that grateful people are happier and more likely to maintain good friendships. A state of gratitude, according to research by the Institute of Heart Math, also improves the heart's rhythmic functioning, which helps us to reduce stress, think more clearly under pressure, and heal physically. It's actually physically impossible to be stressed and thankful at the same time.

I will keep on healing and growing, and my next book is already in the making, as I type these words. It will be a step-by-step guide to optimal health. It will be easy to follow, packed with healing tips and information, for anyone seeking optimal health and vitality.

My own story will continue to evolve, as I believe we will be able to do better as long as we are living this life. My health is still improving, every single month, and I never tire of supporting my process. My joints are still restoring, and my body is still regenerating. I keep setting goals for the future, as there is no finish line.

I am humble to be able to share this story of mine with *you*, and I wish you the best life and the most blessed journey imaginable!

"Thank you, friends, for being in my Tribe.
Thank you, body, for rejuvenating and regenerating, and for always healing on all levels.
Thank you, cells, for being happy, for being healthy and vital.
Thank you, life, for supporting me in everything I do, and for teaching me through my own experiences.
Thank you, nature, for being abundant and perfect.
Thank you for every breath, every smile, and every sunrise.
Thank you for you!
Thank you!"

NOTES:

Hopefully, reading Hilde`s story has inspired you to change your own life for the better. Or maybe you want to inspire someone else. The book; *"Know the Truth and get Healthy"* will be available as an easy to follow step by step guide. The book is packed with information, all from Hilde`s own experience. It will include everything you need to turn your life around.

- ✓ *Healing juice recipes.*
- ✓ *Full menu plan.*
- ✓ *Homemade essential oils recipes.*
- ✓ *Step by step information on healing.*
- ✓ *Meditation exercises.*
- ✓ *Healing crises remedy.*
- ✓ *Breathing exercises.*
- ✓ *Detoxification and regeneration made easy.*
- ✓ *A complete guide from where you are to where you want to be.*

To learn more about Hilde, her work and her services, visit her website. Sign up for her newsletter to receive the latest news and recipes: www.inspiredbyhilde.com

Download the FREE e-book *Notes to Power up* here: http://inspiredbyhilde.com/notes-to-power-up/

Download the FREE e-book *Blessed by Essential oils* here: http://inspiredbyhilde.com/blessed-by-essential-oils/

Hilde has an easy to follow online detoxification program:https://zparkl.com/course/about/2/life-transforming-detoxification-cleansing-program/

Printed in the United States
By Bookmasters

Printed in the United States
By Bookmasters